No Longer
A Child
OF
Promise

No Longer A Child of Promise

A Sequel to
If You Leave This Farm

Amanda Farmer

ARCHWAY
PUBLISHING

Archway Publishing books may be ordered through booksellers or by contacting:

Archway Publishing
1663 Liberty Drive
Bloomington, IN 47403
www.archwaypublishing.com
1 (888) 242-5904

Because of the dynamic nature of the Internet, any web addresses or
links contained in this book may have changed since publication and
may no longer be valid. The views expressed in this work are solely those
of the author and do not necessarily reflect the views of the publisher,
and the publisher hereby disclaims any responsibility for them.

Certain stock imagery © Thinkstock.
Any people depicted in stock imagery provided by Thinkstock are
models, and such images are being used for illustrative purposes only.

ISBN: 978-1-4808-2086-9 (sc)
ISBN: 978-1-4808-2087-6 (hc)
ISBN: 978-1-4808-2088-3 (e)

Library of Congress Control Number: 2015948996

Print information available on the last page.

Archway Publishing rev. date: 8/27/2015

Dedication

This book is dedicated to my brother, Joseph, and to all my nieces and nephews in the next generation for whom I carry a particularly heavy burden. Joseph has supported me and encouraged me throughout this endeavor to share a precautionary tale with others that we hope in some way encourages and warns, while at the same time, provides hope.

I also wish to acknowledge and thank my husband and my daughter for being understanding of the many hours of toil and tears that went into first of all living this heartbreak and then later deciding to write about it.

Disclaimer

The names in this book, as in the first one, have been changed to protect the dignity and privacy of those involved. The area of the setting in Minnesota and the town names and places have also been changed or made ambiguous for the same reason. In telling this story, I acknowledge that these are my recollections of the events and my experience and others may have had a totally different experience or hold a different perspective on these same events. This narrative is based on my life experience and is mostly factual to the extent that telling such a story is possible. This story is not intended to cause stress or harm to any character.

Contents

Preface

No Longer a Child of Promise is the continuation of my personally distinctive story of leaving the farm begun in my first memoir, *If You Leave This Farm ... The Dream Is Destroyed.* My and my brother, Joe's, leaving the farm was not the end of the story and resulted in consequences later down the road that I did not foresee and would never have predicted.

This sequel chronicles the adventures of this young Mennonite lady, who at age twenty-nine, is now free to make her own choices as an adult. But that freedom and joy is tainted by the intertwined and overpowering story of the continued disintegration of her family of origin as a result of unspoken, unrecognized, and unresolved expectations. This is one story of what can happen when one child stays on the farm and others leave to begin a different life. It is a journey of heartache, and in sharing my story, I especially hope that I can prevent other farm or multigenerational business families from traveling into the depths thereof. My hope is that my story will provide insight and understanding into the difficulties that can arise in families who attempt to mingle their personal lives and futures together.

From a different perspective, this memoir is a story of the

triumph of the human spirit in rising above the limitations placed on one by one's family of origin. It is a journey of learning to release the hurt and bitterness that can develop when true reconciliation between close family members seems beyond reach and that Hallmark moment one longs for is never to come.

This book is written especially for those who, with high hopes, set out to make a living by working together with family members and often, employ little thought to the legal and emotional implications that may arise in the future, especially if members want to leave. This is not, however, a book that touches a limited portion of the population. All human beings can relate to the emotional, mental, and spiritual struggles that ensue in the most intimate of human relationships. We all want to be loved and accepted by our families. And we all eventually die. The will is often a taboo subject, and its contents can throw even the most loving of families into turmoil, releasing expectations, hurts, and rivalries that have lain dormant for years.

Chapter 1

Revisiting the Past

At the present time, I have the following children: Paul Reimer, Amanda Reimer, and Joseph Reimer. I intentionally omit all of my children from this, my Last Will and Testament, except for the provisions made for Paul Reimer as set forth herein. The omission of all of my children except for Paul Reimer is not occasioned by accident or mistake and is intentional. My son, Paul Reimer, has stayed with us on the farm and we would not have been able to hold it together and have the type of assets we have today without his dedication and assistance. He is the one that should reap the benefit of his hard work ... All of my clothing, jewelry, ornaments, automobile or automobiles, books, household furniture and furnishings, and personal effects of every kind and nature used about my person or home at the time of my decease I hereby devise ... the same in equal shares to my son, Paul

Reimer, and the issue of my son, Paul Reimer, by right
of representation …

—The Last Will and Testament of Jay Reimer,
March 1995

I stare at the documents in my hand. It is 2008, and I am
reading a signed last will and testament of my father. In
the same package of documents is my mother's will. It is a mirror
image of my father's. No, my parents are not deceased. But rather
they are under a conservatorship during which time all their legal
arrangements have come to light. The shock, the rejection, and
the pain that I feel wash over me and almost take my breath away.
Echoes of the past reverberate in my mind.

It is the summer of 1986. I am twenty-nine years old. I watch
Pappy's retreating back with a sense of despair. His figure, clad in
green cotton pants supported by suspenders over the usual gray
shirt and topped with a Dekalb cap, strides purposefully and deter-
minedly away from me toward his truck. I do not know this man or
respect him any longer. I am at the end of my rope. I have no desire
to do anything. I just cannot go on. I sit on a straw bale on this warm
sunny summer day for several minutes and try to decide what to do.
I am sick to my stomach. The black cloud that always threatens to
overtake me descends like a shroud around me. *I just want to die.*

I had not planned to leave my job as the dairy herdsperson
on my father's farm just yet. I have not finished getting the cow
records up to snuff. Now, I no longer care. My shoulders droop,
and I walk slowly to the two-story white farmhouse. I tread softly
through the kitchen, turn right, and head up the stairs to my
bedroom. Mama is sleeping on the couch downstairs in the living
room after a night of work at the hospital as a nurse. I pull out
Mama's old suitcase that is stored in my closet and begin to throw

the basic items that I will need into it. Then I sit on my bed for minutes at a time, trying to decide if I can really go through with this. My mind is in turmoil. Every muscle in my body contracts as fear grips me. I finally snap the suitcase shut and tiptoe down the stairs to the kitchen. Mama is still asleep.

"Mama," I say as I detour to the living room door. Her eyes flicker open. "I'm leaving."

Without giving her time to respond, I spin, pick up the suitcase, and stride quickly toward my car. I waste no time in throwing the suitcase into the backseat and plunking myself behind the wheel. I do not want to allow Mama any time to try to stop me. Having been jerked from her slumber by my sudden announcement, Mama gathers herself up to follow me. I see her standing with her arms hanging limply at her sides on the mudroom entry steps as I drive away. Her Mennonite-style dress covered with an apron and her uncombed hair wave in the breeze as she gazes after me in bewilderment.

Just a little over a year later, in 1987, I am jolted awake at 2:30 p.m. from my day sleeping after a previous night shift at the hospital as a nurse by the ringing of the telephone.

"Hello," I groggily intone into the phone.

"This is Joe. Will you come and get me? I need to get out of here."

Now I am wide awake. My mind races. I am torn as to how to respond.

"I don't really want to get involved," I tell him.

"Just get me out of here and give me a ride to the bus station. I can take care of myself from there," he pleads.

I pause while I try to decide what to do. I know how hard it was for me to leave and how everyone was reluctant to help for fear of Pappy. *If I don't help him, no one else is going to. Certainly, Joe deserves to escape as much as I did.*

"All right," I give in. "I'll come and get you tomorrow afternoon."

I am shaking as I hang up the phone. I know there will be ramifications for helping him. I also have no idea if Pappy and Mama are even aware of his plan to leave.

I try to swallow the lump in my throat as I drive up the long driveway and park beside the old box-shaped farmhouse the next afternoon. I am queasy and lightheaded. Joe, a well-built muscular young man, comes out of his bedroom and down the stairs, carrying the infamous suitcase. Pappy and Mama sit in the living room sobbing. The tears start to roll down my cheeks too. I feel sorry for these people who are my parents. They are crying because their children have "abandoned" them. They are heartbroken that their dream of us all farming together has been totally dashed.

"How are we going to make it now?" is their plaintive question to us.

I do not answer. There is no benefit in pointing out that their inability to transition from treating us like children to treating us like adults has brought about this result. I need to get out of here.

"Come on. Let's go." I nod at Joe, my twenty-nine-year-old brother, and jerk my head toward the door. We climb into the car and drive away.

Joe and I have both chosen to leave the unrealistic demands of life on the farm under our father's tight control. We are leaving him and our older brother, Paul, to manage and work the farm alone. Yes, my father told me and Joe that if we left the farm, we would not get anything from it, but leaving the farm to Paul is a different thing than totally disinheriting us. How had we come to this point as a family that my parents' final message to us is one of abandonment and of completely disowning us?

Chapter 2
BUILDING A NEW LIFE

*L*ife for me settles into a pattern during 1988. I visit the folks and their greater-than-one-thousand-acre farm three to four days each month with the intention of helping with the various farm chores. There are two hundred dairy cows to milk, baby calves and young heifers to care for, and crops to harvest. Then I return to my separate world in the bustling city of Superior, Minnesota. I hear stories of hired men who last only a few weeks and then move on. The standard joke in the community is that it takes two hired men to replace one woman (me) and none of them stay. At the hospital, where I work the night shift, I struggle to become competent as a nurse. Most of the time, I feel like I am disorganized and can't keep up with the pace. This I find discouraging, as I was confident, proficient, and experienced in my job as a herdsman.

I find living in the city alone as a Mennonite to be an extremely lonely experience. I write in my diary one day, "I am trying to stifle my overwhelming pain of being alone." I long to have a companion with whom to share my life. Most of all, I just want to be *normal* and accepted for who I am. A certain emptiness, a certain feeling of disconnectedness from everyone, produces a low-level depression that I can never quite shake.

I continue to attend Moorland Mennonite church, a small church of about forty members, on Sunday mornings. There, I develop a close friendship with the new school teacher who has been hired to teach the children of the small Mennonite group. We spend many happy hours hanging out and doing things together. But I always feel like I carry around a certain shame, a certain stigma in the Mennonite church because of my father's independent, uncompromising positions on various issues and Mama's critical tongue. Such a reputation is not something that stays confined to the local church but often gets spread throughout the network of other conservative Mennonite churches in the United States. I begin to realize that at the age of thirty-one, my chances of an upstanding Mennonite man wanting to court me are slim to none, though I am still committed to the teachings of the conservative church.

My adventurous side, which has been suppressed for years, begins to emerge. I book a two-week trip with a Mennonite tour group to Israel, Switzerland, and England.

Cold, zero-degree air stings my cheeks, but the skies are blue and the sun illuminates the day as my Mennonite schoolteacher friend deposits me at the airport at 6:45 a.m. on February 29, 1988. The only excitement at this airport is a mouse running around. Everyone sits there frozen and terrified as the little creature scurries around. I am amused but finally get out of my chair and stomp on the offending rodent. I board a little prop jet at 7:30 a.m. It is a nice, smooth takeoff for my first airplane ride ever. We land at 9:00 a.m. in St. Louis, Missouri. *What a confusing place.*

I am finally able to navigate the labyrinth and find the correct terminal.

JFK airport in New York sports skies that hang heavy with dark clouds when we descend at 2:00 p.m. EST. I find the baggage area without a problem and retrieve my luggage. Aimlessly, I wander out into the street and scan the honking taxis, numerous buses, and cars. *How am I supposed to get to Sabena Airlines?* I have never done anything like this before, and I am alone in a bustling big world. One of the little shuttle buses stops in front of me. I might as well get on. This bus goes as far as British Airways before it stops, and we are all told that we need to get off. The only thing left to do is get onto another bus. In the rush and commotion, I sit down beside a fellow who directs a question to me, "Are you going on the Klassen Tour?"

After all, I am dressed as a Mennonite and that is how Mennonites recognize each other. "Yes," I respond, "but I have no idea what I am doing."

"We need to get off at the American Airlines terminal," he instructs me.

Okay. So, at least, now I have someone to be lost with. We wander around until we come upon a group of Mennonites. What a relief. Wesley Klassen, the Canadian tour group leader, and the rest of the Canadians do not arrive until around 4:00 p.m. Then things get underway. We begin by boarding a Boeing 747 at 6:00 p.m. EST and are ready for takeoff by 7:00 p.m. It is dark outside, and the city is an amazing maze of lights. I am excited to begin this adventure now that I have a group of fellow Mennonites to hang out with.

It is cloudy, muggy, and sixty-six degrees in Tel Aviv, Israel, when we land there the following day. Tel Aviv is a confusing array of people. There are people everywhere, and most of them are foreigners. We board a modern tour bus for the trip to the hotel in Nathanya. Darkness has slid over the land by the time we arrive. Ruby Herr and I have been assigned a room together with a balcony that overlooks the Mediterranean Sea. I love the sound of the sea and the feel of the cool breeze that wafts our way. I see we have company here too—another mouse. The countryside in Israel is cluttered with piles of destroyed and falling down buildings from the various clashes and wars.

The fourth day of our tour in Israel starts out as all of them do and is representative of our busy days. We arise at 6:00 a.m., breakfast is served at 7:00, and we are eagerly waiting to board the bus by 8:00. Our itinerary today lists Capernaum as our first stop. We are to see the church of the Beatitudes. Seated under an outdoor grove of palm trees, one of the male members of the group reads the Sermon on the Mount from Matthew's Gospel while we breathe in the air of this land where Jesus walked. We then travel on by bus to Tabgha to view the Church of the Loaves and Fishes. Touring the ruins of the city of Capernaum comes next, before we board a sailboat for a crossing of the Sea of Galilee. It is sunny but breezy and cool. We sail over the water as the mast billows ahead of the wind. The sailors drop the sails and throw out the anchor in the middle of the lake, allowing us to sing some songs and read another passage of scripture. The boat docks at Ein Gev around noon. We are to visit to a kibitz, a communal farm or settlement in Israel usually based on agriculture. This one runs the boat line, has a restaurant for tourists, and also has a four-hundred-cow dairy operation (just like home) besides growing tropical fruit. It is warm here. The guide tells us that it is very hot most of the time. We dine in the restaurant where we are served whole cooked fish with the head, eyes, and all. I am not sure I care for my fish staring back at me while I eat him.

After leaving Ein Gev, we continue our journey toward Mount Tabor, the Mount of Transfiguration in the Bible. We stop along the way at the Jordan River. By now, it is midafternoon, and the weather has turned cool and cloudy. Because of the narrow, steep mountainous road, we exit the bus and climb into taxis for a thrilling, scary ride up the mountain road, which has numerous hairpin turns, resulting in a few close calls with the taxis coming down. Our destination is the church built on the Mount of Transfiguration. We are able to look out over the Valley of Jezreel from the balcony. The Jezreel Valley is home to some of the most fertile farmland in Israel. It is the agricultural heartland of the country, an area rich in natural springs and beauty. It is getting dark and starting to rain as we reboard the bus for the drive to Jerusalem. Because of the tensions and unrest around Shekhem, we detour to the north and travel along the Jordan River on the West Bank. We can see the country of Jordan from the bus. We also see some soldiers, but otherwise, we have a good, though long and tiresome, trip through Jericho to Jerusalem to St. George Hotel. A delicious dinner of stuffed eggplant, beans, chicken, and rice awaits us.

Traveling back in time to the area of Jesus's death and resurrection on the sixth day of our trip is probably the most meaningful part of this experience for me. We pose for a group picture in front of the St. George Hotel in Jerusalem and then are ready to board the bus by 8:00 a.m. We begin our day with a tour of the old city of Jerusalem. I, as well as some others, decide to pay for a camel ride. It is basically an experience in hanging on tight as the camel rocks to its feet, takes a few steps, and then is instructed to lie down again so I can get off. From Old Jerusalem, we visit the church built over the place where Jesus taught his disciples the Lord's Prayer. "Our Father which art in Heaven, Hallowed be Thy Name, thy Kingdom Come ..." (Luke 11:2 KJV)—we say together before continuing on to the Garden Tomb, the Hill of the Skull, and the place where Jesus was probably crucified. Solemnly, we each peek into the empty tomb and then gather to sing a couple of songs a cappella, including, "Christ Arose" by songwriter Robert Lowry (1874) and "At Calvary" by William R. Newell (1895). A short service follows in the Garden of Gethsemane where our tour guide reads the biblical story of the resurrection. We lift our voices in worship with a final song, "My Savior's Love" by Charles H. Gabriel (1905). In the afternoon, we stroll through an underground system of aqueducts and pass through the area where the soldiers scourged Jesus. We continue into the courtyard where Pilate tried and the people condemned Jesus with their cries of "Crucify Him, Crucify Him" (Luke 23:21 KJV). We finish by treading the Via Delarosa, or the Way of Sorrow, to the cross.

We return to the hotel at 6:15 p.m. I am starting to feel quite comfortable and relaxed with these people I am traveling with. They have become like a big family to me, and I have put away my lifelong inhibitions. Ruby, my roommate, and I decide to go exploring out through the hotel room window by way of the roof. We visit a couple of other young ladies by our strange method of travel. After supper, we sit around and relate the events of the day. Outside in the hall, it sounds like a party. When we crack open the door, we discover that some of our group has dressed up and are blowing the shepherd's bugle and imitating the events of the day. We laugh until the tears course down our cheeks.

The days fly by way too fast while we try to take in all the sights, and far too soon, it is time to move on to Europe. March 8, day nine, finds us in Switzerland, the ancestral origin of the Anabaptist groups from which Amish, Mennonites, and Hutterites trace their heritage. All we have to eat for breakfast is bread, jelly, and tea. We start off our day traveling toward Bern. White snowflakes are cascading from the sky, whitewashing the landscape. Our bus driver starts our route backward in the hope that by afternoon, the mountain roads will have melted. The sun soon breaks through, and the sparkles on the whiteness of the land offer breathtaking beauty. We stop first to visit the oldest Mennonite church at Langnau. We chat with the pastor and sing, "Gott ist die Liebe" (August Rische). Our next stop is at a small Anabaptist church that used to be disguised as a barn to hide its presence from the authorities during the early reformation in the 1600s. We continue on to see the castle at Sumiswald where the Anabaptists were imprisoned and cruelly tortured for their beliefs, the primary belief being the need to be baptized as an adult on confession of faith. For the Anabaptists of that day, this meant being rebaptized, as they had all been baptized as infants in the state church of that time.

The bus wheels whirl around with a loud whine but no forward motion when the driver tries to begin his ascent on the road to the castle. It is too slippery for the bus so we all trudge up. Soon, snowballs are flying and laughter rings in the air. The steps to the castle are many, and we climb a portion where it is very narrow. We need flashlights to find our way in the darkness. I find myself clinging to the handrail. We halt at the torture chamber. Chills run up my spine as we continue to the top. This is eerie and creepy. The bus driver has put chains on the bus and awaits us at the top when we are ready to depart. The only snag in the plan is that he needs to back the bus down the steep hill, as there is no place to turn around.

We do some more sightseeing on the drive from the castle to Gundelwald. The plan is to ride a chairlift to the top of the mountain at this ski resort. We buy our tickets, wrap ourselves in trench coats for warmth, and get on. Ruby and I huddle together for the thirty-minute trip to the top. It is about two miles. The temperature is in the twenties, and the wind turns our cheeks rosy red, but what a wonderful, breathtaking view of the chalets covered in four feet of sparkling white snow! We eat our lunch in the restaurant at the top. It takes us two and a half hours to ascend, eat, and return to the bottom. We are treated to some more of God's beautiful scenery on the way back to the hotel. It is snowing again too, but snow cannot begin to destroy the comradery that has developed among the young single ladies.

The last country on our itinerary is England. We travel by train across the French countryside from Switzerland to Boulogne, France, where we board a hovercraft to cross the English Channel to Dover, England.

The last day of our excursion dawns sunny and cool with the temperature around 50 degrees. Our hotel is located in the King's Cross area of London. The bus takes us through Westminster, around Hyde Park, and past Speaker's Corner. The royal soldiers in their red and black uniforms marching like wooden toy soldiers are getting ready for exercises during the Queen's birthday. We all gawk out the window as we drive past Buckingham Palace where the queen makes her home. There is no sign of the queen though. We pause in front of parliament just long enough to snap a picture. As we drive on, our attention is directed toward St. Thomas Hospital where Florence Nightingale worked and later Droning, where Margaret Thatcher lived.

One of our other stops is the Tower of London. Here, thousands of people were imprisoned by King Henry VIII as "enemies of the state" and later beheaded by him. Ruby and I take a tour of the museum with the armor and decide to explore the spiral stairs to the tower. We begin to wonder if we will have permanent residence in the tower as we are having a hard time finding our way down again. As this is our final day of this trip, we return to the hotel by 4:00 p.m., where our thirty-member tour group has a final happy and tearful get-together.

I go home energized by the fellowship and the enjoyment I experienced exploring with this group. I have made a friend for life with Ruby, my roommate. Additionally, walking where Jesus walked has a profound impact on my faith. I renew my commitment to follow Christ in my decisions of life.

A couple of months later, I buy another plane ticket, this time to Arkansas to visit Joe for a week. He has been living with a Mennonite minister's family who have basically adopted him. In his own words, here is his account of those first few years after leaving home.

> After my first ride on a Greyhound bus, I decided that there wouldn't be many more! It took three times as long to get somewhere as it should have. Standing at a deserted bus stop at Anderson, Missouri, I think, was the loneliest night of my life—waiting for someone I didn't know to come and pick me up. There would be many more times of trusting people I didn't know.
>
> Emotionally, this was a very difficult time. I had to transition overnight from being a "piece of machinery" to being a human being. That is no easy task in a world where work is just supposed to be a small part of the rest of life. I had never talked to girls before—at least not one-on-one. But the hardest thing to deal with was the rejection that my parents considered me to be a disappointment! There was no joy found by them in my presence. Just the frown of disapproval and the ultimate rejection manifested in being told "if you don't like the way I do things, you can leave."
>
> I only worked on chicken cage building jobs for

about a month. Over Thanksgiving, everyone else went home. I had no home to go to. Then a man from Arkansas asked if I would be willing to come help him in Arkansas. Since the cage job was ending, I went. His parents (a Mennonite minister and his wife) picked me up—after some miscommunication and chaos until they got to the right bus stop. I lived with them for about two years. The minister also signed for me to get my first car. I was ashamed and embarrassed because most guys my age (thirty years old) had been through several cars by this time.

The work that the father and son gave me was quite sporadic and not very steady so I went to work in a sawmill/pallet shop. I worked there for six years. I joined the Beachy Amish church during this time and was able to buy a house trailer and ten acres of land. I ran with the "young" folks for a while but in time, realized I didn't fit in anywhere. I also tried asking some girls on dates. Two refused, and one didn't work out. I realized that I was being prejudged based on my father's reputation and on his telling everyone that I was a rebel. The whispers were floating around to any prospective dates. "Better be careful—Joe had a bad home life—like father, like son you know."

Joe greets me at the airport on my arrival with a stiff-armed hug. Hugging for us is a new and awkward behavior, but we are trying to learn to express emotion like normal people. We spend several happy days together touring Arkansas. I am pleased to see that he has blossomed on his own. He is no longer the timid, unsure brother that I knew, but a confident man who is not afraid to speak his mind. I thank the Lord for the kind, loving Mennonite minister and his wife who have taken Joe into their home and helped him get his feet on the ground.

Finally accepting that I am probably never going to get married, I make a conscious decision to move on with my life alone. My main goals are to explore the world and make a difference in it. A first step toward my new direction in January of this year, 1989, is to go looking for a house to buy. I find a cozy two-bedroom ranch home with no basement nestled on a cul-de-sac in Sun Prairie, Minnesota. I fall in love with it.

Moving day is spent unpacking and organizing my first little home. In the evening, I need to head out to a research class. I am continuing to take classes at the state university in my quest for a four-year degree. By ten o'clock in the evening, I am home and snuggled into my warm, wavy waterbed. As my eyelids begin to drift shut, I feel the rumble of an approaching train. The rhythmic shaking is followed by a long, shrill whistle just outside my bedroom window. Maybe, symbolically, it is proclaiming the beginning of another segment of my life's journey.

In spite of the nearness of the railroad tracks with the ear-splitting whistle at the most unexpected hours, I love my new home in Sun Prairie. Long walks through the woods at a nearby county park rejuvenate me and lift my spirits. Henceforth, I am drawn to hiking in the woods at least once or twice a week. But this warm, sunny June day will be perfect for a different kind of adventure. Horses have always fascinated me, but I have never been able to own one. My father always said that they were just hay burners and didn't make any money. I still have no place to keep a horse of my own, but I have found an arena just a few miles west of Sun Prairie that offers horseback lessons. My plan is to pedal over to the horse stables today for my lesson. That way, I can satisfy my passion for bike riding on the way to my equestrian pursuits.

Since none of these activities that I have come to enjoy is particularly easily done in a skirt, I have arrived at a compromise with my conscience. I have begun to sew culottes. I wear them around the house almost continually now instead of the cape dresses prescribed for Mennonite women. The benefit is that I no longer need to worry about my dress being up over my head at the most inappropriate times.

By afternoon, I am ready for a nap. Excitement, however, prevents me from reaching the land of doze as I roll over in my mind the escapade that awaits me tonight. I am scheduled for a ride-along with the area city police department. I have always been drawn toward and excited by the drama of police work. I am pretty sure that if I had not been born a Mennonite woman, my choice of occupation would have been law enforcement. I made the connection for this experience through a coworker, who has a friend on the police force. I meet up with my coworker for supper and then head to the law enforcement center to be paired with an officer. "Being in the fishbowl" is how the policeman describes his work shift. I know exactly what he means, for I feel like I live in a fishbowl also. All heads turn every time a conservative Mennonite or Amish woman walks by. I finally crash into bed at 6:00 a.m. after a stimulating night of chasing the bad guys. I could do that every night.

Now that I feel released from the constant critical eye that followed me at home, I am enthralled with trying new things and enjoying life. I return to my desire from my early twenties to work in the field of emergency medicine by signing up for the first responder class to be held in the fall. Once I complete it, I join the Sun Prairie First Responders. I also try roller skating in the fall and downhill skiing in the winter. And I begin to spend time at my coworker's house, watching home videos.

Ding dong! Ding dong! I open my eyes and jump out of bed. *Who is ringing my doorbell at eight o'clock on Sunday morning?* As I swing open the door, I inwardly groan. A twenty-something average-build young man dressed in Sunday-go-to-meetin' clothes stands at my door. I press my lips into a firm line and narrow my eyes as I meet his.

"What do you want, Kirk?"

"I thought I would come by and see if I could go along to church with you today," he announces.

I turn my body away from him while continuing to hold the door open. "Come in then."

I am irritated, but I don't really want to hurt his feelings. I leave him seated on the couch while I go to get dressed. Inwardly, I fume while I get ready. *How inconsiderate does a guy need to be to just show up on my doorstep without even calling?* I suck a breath in and let it out slowly to calm myself. I will put up with this for today. Then I need to have a serious talk with this man. I have no attraction to the guy and do not wish to pursue a relationship with him. He is younger than I am and does not have any idea what he wants to do in life while I am established in my career. However, he is persistent and I know he wants a relationship.

I met Kirk a few weeks ago at college. He told me initially that he just wanted to find out more about the Mennonites, and I have taken him along to church a couple of times. Just a couple of weeks ago, though, he called and asked if he could come over one evening at seven o'clock. I hesitated and then reluctantly agreed. Seven o'clock came and went, and he still had not shown up. I was annoyed. I do not appreciate people who waste my time by keeping me waiting while not even bothering to call. I decided to forget about Kirk and to make the best of my remaining evening by going for a walk at the county park. However, when I returned an hour later, Kirk was perched on my doorstep. Interestingly, he has also made a visit alone to the farm to see Pappy and Mama. From my perspective, he is way too eager to join the Mennonites just to be able to attract me. And this being chummy with my parents does not ingratiate him to me.

A couple of days later, I gather up my nerve and call him.

"Please don't call me again. We are from two different worlds and at totally different stations in life."

I purposely forget to mention that I really don't like him. Being somewhat clueless, he tries to contact me again several times. I learn to hang up the phone when I hear his voice. I subsequently hear from Mama that he still visits them occasionally over the next couple of years. This encounter has shown me that apparently, I do have the ability to attract a guy, just not one that I am interested in.

It is the time of year for the Indiana Mennonite Fellowship meetings. Mama asks me if I will come and help with the milking, other farm work, and cooking for Paul while Pappy and she go to the meetings. I am not particularly thrilled about the idea, but I still feel obligated to help as much as I can. They do need time away too. I schedule my vacation from the hospital for August 16 through 27. That way, I can help for the preceding five days necessary and still make it back home in time to meet up with a tour group from my workplace. I am looking forward to going on a six-day trip into the Boundary Waters Canoe Area of Minnesota in late August.

Pappy and Mama left yesterday. I groan when the alarm goes off. It has been a long time since I crawled out of bed at four o'clock in the morning. I have still been coming every other weekend or so to help milk and take care of the calves, but I don't usually get up until six o'clock. I let Pappy, Paul, and whatever hired man they might have at the moment do the getting up early. The deliciousness of sleep has begun to erode my guilt-induced drive to continue to try to prove my worth as a good daughter and sister. Ultimately, the only reason I am here this week is that I still believe that the ticket to any acceptance in this family is based on my willingness to contribute to the workload.

The eastern sky is starting to lighten as I begin the milking chores. *Just like old times.* The smell of freshly mown hay hangs in the still morning air and touches my nostrils as I walk to the house after milking. I stir up the usual oatmeal breakfast for Paul. I'm not really sure why I even agreed to do this. Since the departures of both Joe and me from the farm, Paul pretty much ignores me. He acts like I am in the way. He talks to me in grunts and only when truly necessary. We eat breakfast in silence, and then he is gone.

As I wash the dishes, I hear the tractor come roaring around by the garage. The baler is hooked behind and ready to go. Soon Paul's tall, thin frame appears in the doorway. His green eyes are piercing, and his body is always in motion, radiating nervous energy.

"So are you going to drive the baler for me?" The words are thrown my way.

I am startled by his impromptu request, but I am here to help so I nod.

The sun beats upon my head as the tractor creeps along the disappearing row of sun-dried hay. I rock rhythmically back and forth as the machine gobbles up the fodder into its mouth and pounds it into little green bales. The baler then spits them out the back onto the ground. Paul speeds around behind me with the bale wagon, picking up the cow food for the winter and delivering it to the barn. Everything is still done at high speed. As we work, my thoughts wander. *I wonder when he is going to get over being mad at me for leaving the farm. I wish we could just move on and be friends again.* My face and arms turn a deep shade of brown from the mixture of sun and dirt. By one o'clock in the afternoon, we are both getting hungry so it is time to stop and make dinner.

Later in the day, I pour out the discarded antibiotic-treated milk from the previous milking into buckets and add water. As I do so, thirty hungry calves sing together for their supper in a not-so-harmonious chorus. I came out as soon as the dinner dishes were washed and put away to feed the calves, a job that needs to be done before I milk. It takes an hour to complete the task of lugging heavy buckets back and forth and distributing the hay to each calf hutch—a three-sided rectangular box, which each calf lives in separately. Then it is time to milk again. I am beginning to feel the old, overwhelming frustration and weariness from all the work, and this is only the first day. I count the days until Pappy and Mama return. I do not miss this rat race of a life. At least I have my next adventure to look forward to. Canoeing into the wilderness will be another new experience for me.

The sky is gray above the towering pines that line the smoothly flowing river as we launch thirteen canoes into the Boundary Waters Canoe Area of Northern Minnesota. Twenty-six of us are cocooned in our rain parkas as the cold raindrops make rivers of a different kind over our shoulders. In my culottes, rain parka, and Mennonite head covering, I look vastly different from the rest of the group in their shorts and T-shirts. I am paired with Susan as my canoe partner, neither of us having much experience in this skill of making a canoe go straight. It is not a very nice day to set off into the wilderness, but the rain stops in a couple of hours and we are left with only low-hanging clouds.

I had left the farm on Sunday evening and rushed home to get packed for my trip. Monday morning brought me to Superior, Minnesota, to meet the rest of the Boundary Waters–bound group, and we were soon on the road for the eight-hour drive to Grand Marais, Minnesota. Grand Marais is the last town before no-man's-land when heading north in Minnesota. We then begin the drive to the outfitter's lodge up the Gunflint Trail. The journey is punctuated by the sun's rays rhythmically slapping the towering evergreens that line the narrow road. As the sun drifts below the western horizon, we arrive at the end of civilization. I am too excited to sleep well in the bunkhouse and am very disappointed to wake up to the sound of rain upon our roof.

But rain is not about to stop this group, and we are being carried away from everyday comforts by 8:00 a.m. All that is heard for a few hours is the slap of the canoe paddles and some bantering going back and forth between the thirteen canoes in our group. Then it is time to portage. This means that the river is too rocky or too shallow for the canoes to navigate so we must pick up our canoes and our packs and carry them through the trees to the river opening on the other side of the dangerous section. Wet shoes are an expected part of portaging, but the rain has mixed up a nice paste of mud for all of our feet. We laugh and forget about trying to be clean and unsoiled. Working together, we successfully traverse four portages and many miles of canoeing throughout the day. I do not mind the work of portaging. All those years of lifting hay bales and calves has prepared me well for the challenge of wilderness living. I love the outdoors and the solitude—no motors, no phone, no anything except miles of God's creation.

Our guide manages to overturn his canoe in some rapids, dumping his young son into the cold water, but other than that mishap, the day flows along nicely. We find an unoccupied camp-site and are able to set up our tents by midafternoon. Then it is time to relax, cook over the fire, and tell stories by firelight. Most of the group is single, like me, and I feel happy and content to sit and listen to the chatter around the campfire. I especially love to hear the far-off mournful cry of the loons as I lay upon my hard sleeping bag, waiting for the sleepy man to come.

Each day, we pack up and move on to a different camping spot. The beauty is breathtaking. I love the peace in the stillness of this place far from the bustle of the city. On our last day, Friday, the group decides not to break camp but to spend the day hiking around the various islands in the middle of the vast lake that we are camped along. Others spend the time fishing or relaxing. We return to our camp for the evening meal and start a fire. As the sun sinks into the western sky, someone decides that we should go hiking on an island in the moonlight. I am still young and have the adventurous spirit, so I go along with this idea. Stumbling through the brush in the dark, though, with thoughts of bears out there somewhere is more than enough to make me wonder if this was really such a good idea. It does, however, cause a spike in my adrenaline and satisfies my need for adventure for a short while.

As I enter the next year, 1990, I begin to think about dedi-cating my nursing skills to the service of others in less fortunate situations. I would be available to go into full-time missions once I completed my four-year nursing degree. For now, though, I decide to participate in a short-term mission trip to see if foreign mission work is truly my calling. A coworker has been talking about serving with a Christian organization called Mercy Ships. Mercy Ships owns and sponsors a hospital ship, the *Anastasia*, which sails around the world to third-world countries. The organization provides surgeries to the poor who have no access to medical care and could not afford it even if they did. I eagerly sign on as a nurse for a three-week trip to the Dominican Republic in the spring and begin making plans.

My coworker and I leave on the morning of February 24 for the airport in Superior, Minnesota. We are to fly out at 8:30 a.m., but because of bad weather and plane problems, we do not take off until 11:30 a.m. This starts a cascade of misadventure and missed connections in our journey. We barely make our flight in St. Louis after running at top speed from one terminal to another. However, our effort proves to be useless as we miss the plane to San Domingo from Miami. This mischance leaves two non-Spanish-speaking young ladies on their own in a strange country the next day when we finally arrive in San Domingo. No one is there to meet us. I am so glad that we have each other. Getting into a "taxi" with two strange men with the hope that it will take us where we need to go is probably not the smartest move on our part, but we don't know what else to do. The driver does deliver us without incident to the ship later in the day.

The surgeons on the ship are performing mostly cleft lip and hernia repairs for children. Working in the stuffy, crowded ward, I find both rewarding and frustrating. I cannot communicate in the language of the people, and the nursing care seems totally disorganized. All the supplies are donated and of many different brands. There are nurses from forty different countries on board the ship, and no one seems to be in charge. But the people are truly grateful for all the help that we give them. By the end of my three weeks, I have decided that this is not the life for me. It has been an eye-opening experience but is far too hectic for this regimented person. I return on March 17, wondering what my next step in life should be.

A week before I left for the Dominican Republic, I had been approached by a person from a newer Mennonite Fellowship in Superior, asking me if I would be willing to take on a roommate. She knew of a young lady who wanted to move to the Superior area but needed a place to live. I did have an extra bedroom and could use the help with paying the mortgage. And thus Fran came to live with me.

Fran, a short, lively, petite little gal, and I hit it off from the beginning and soon become good friends. We talk easily together. One evening, after returning from my adventure with Mercy Ships, I jokingly tell her that I am going to someday place an ad in the personals column of the Superior regional newspaper just to see what kind of replies I'd get. I have been reading the personals fairly regularly over the last few months, picking out ads of interest and then throwing them away after a couple of weeks. She laughs and encourages me to go for it. And thus in late March of 1990, I place an ad.

> 32 year old NBM SWF looking for companionship and/or someone to share some good times with. This person must be a single widower or a NBM SWM between 28–38 years of age who values Christianity and uses it as a basis for his morality. Must also have

a good sense of humor and be able to relax enough to enjoy life. I am independent, adventuresome, and love the outdoors. I enjoy most any outdoor activity but biking and hiking are my favorites. Looking for someone who is open, honest, caring, and able to accept others the way they are.

I pull out a large envelope from my post office box a few weeks later. The return address is that of *Superior News*. I eagerly rip it open. Inside are nine letters from different men all addressed to Post Office Box 25. I like that this process is blinded; none of the men know who I am. I can answer any of them I want or ignore them all if I so choose. I settle into my recliner when I get home to read. I eliminate several on the first reading—he smokes, he's older than thirty-eight, he's divorced. One man goes on and on about how "some women will go out for a while and think nothing of dropping a man and going out with another guy. I know you wouldn't do that." *I am already feeling trapped, and I haven't even met the man.* He signs his letter "Love." *That's a wee bit much for an introductory letter.* One letter in particular, I find strange. The man wants to play this secret game.

"From now on, I want you to address me as 'Pen Pal.' That way you don't know my name, yet I have a title. I'm going to give you a message to leave on a friend's answering machine. He knows nothing about this, but next week, I'll ask him if he got a message like 'Oh, I'm sorry, I got the wrong number. I was calling my Pen Pal.' If when I ask him if he ever heard this message and he gives it to me, I will then give you my number."

Okay. This guy is either married or into keeping secrets. He certainly doesn't sound open and honest to me.

I finally pick out three letters that seem to provide possible candidates. But I am particularly drawn to one letter. The man presents himself in a straightforward, honest, unassuming manner.

> Hello, I have been reading your ad ever since it came out. I still don't know that writing you is right. You seem to have a very specific person in mind and I don't know if I am inside your parameters or not. I do enjoy the outdoors; biking and hiking are great fun. I have never been married and am a white male, age 34. I am a Christian (Lutheran) and enjoy my involvement in the church. I am a member of my church's council and attend services regularly. I think I am caring and honest and other people seem to think so too. I like to think I can take people for what they are. Yet, I think that is probably something others have to judge in me or you. It's not something a person can judge about themselves. So far so good. _Perhaps!_ Now for the part that has me stumped. If you ask anyone if I know how to relax enough to enjoy life, they would probably say that I don't and I guess they would probably be right. I need someone to help me relax and not take things so serious. Just a little about myself. (If you are still reading.) I am 6'4" tall, slim looking even at 220 lbs. It's the height. Brown hair, blue eyes, and 34 years old as stated. I am a nonsmoker and very light social drinker and <u>I seek the same.</u> I enjoy animals and I am currently owned by a cat. I enjoy a good non-horror movie and dining out but they are a lot more fun if done with someone. I enjoy building clocks and have been known to chase a train or two. If after reading this you think I have made it inside your parameters, you can give me a call. Usually home by 9:00 p.m.

Home sooner most days but to be safe, I am home by then most nights. We can talk and see what happens from there. Thank you very much for your time. Thanks. Gordon

I lay the letters aside for the moment. I need to think and pray about this before I actually make up my mind to contact any of them. I decide to take the letters along to work and let some of my coworkers read them. I hope they will give me their input. I have no problem getting them interested in my potential love life. The consensus is that I should contact Gordon.

I still am not sure that I have any intention of really making any contact, but I am intrigued. If I am having any thoughts of calling him, I need to find out something about him. I am not about to go out with a strange man without doing a little research first. All I have is a phone number and a first name—not a lot to go on. I thumb through the local phone book, looking for the prefix of the phone number in his letter. There it is. The prefix is for Algoma, a small town about thirty-five miles east of Sun Prairie, so I should be able to go through that section of the phone book until I find the number. With a shaking hand, I run my finger down the list of numbers. I have not even spent fifteen minutes, and presto, there it is. Farmer Electric is the name attached with the number. I have hit pay dirt. Now I know where Gordon lives, his last name, and apparently, his occupation as well. Armed with this information, I begin to inquire at work if anyone knows the man. It does not take me long to find a nurse who goes to church with him.

"He's a great guy. You can't go wrong," she insists.

Friday, on my day off, I turn the issue over and over in my mind. *Should I call him, or shouldn't I?* Finally, with shaking hands, I take a deep breath and dial the number.

"Hello?" he answers almost immediately. His voice is strong, confident, and pleasant.

We chat for a while, and I roll around in my mind if I should tell him that I am Mennonite. I don't really want him to be shocked out of his mind when he sees me. We agree to meet at Perkins Restaurant in Superior, a neutral place, the following Sunday.

"And you'll recognize me by the little white cap I wear and my dress. I'm Mennonite."

He hesitates a moment and then says, "I don't really know much about Mennonites, but I'll see you then."

He tells me later that if it hadn't been for the promise that he had made to himself when he began placing personal ads and now in answering them to take out any lady who responded to his contacts, he would not have shown up. To himself, he said, "This is going to be one fast lunch."

The man who steps out of the old blue dual-wheel pickup truck is dressed in a blue shirt and blue jeans. I am awestruck. Tall, dark, and handsome would not be an overstatement. As we chat over our meal, I discover that we have a lot in common. His mother is a nurse. My mother is a nurse. His father is a farmer. My father is a farmer. There are three children in each family: older brother, middle daughter, younger brother. We have similar values. I can't quite believe it. Before I know it, we are walking the trails in the county park, whiling away the afternoon talking. I go home energized. Wow! But what do I do with all these feelings? My brain is twirling with conflicting thoughts. *Do I dare go out with him again?*

I roll out early on the waves of my waterbed. The air is hot, and the clouds hang heavy, but my mood is soaring. Love is exhilarating. I want to get an early start driving to the farm. Pappy and Mama plan to go to Wisconsin tomorrow, and in response to their asking, I have agreed to help this weekend with the chores while they get away. I am happy, and I think about the past weeks as I drive. Last Sunday, Gordon and I rode our bikes along the bicycle trail from Superior to a small town ten miles north and then had a picnic for our second date. And this week, I got two letters from him. I said "yes" to going out again with him to his favorite spot above the bluffs along the Mississippi River next Sunday. Then he asked me if I wanted to go to a Red Skelton concert with him on June 13. He does not seem to mind that I dress differently from all the other women he has ever dated, although he has told me that he has no desire to ever become Mennonite. For now, this dating relationship is our little secret. I have no intentions of telling Pappy and Mama.

There are calves waiting to be photographed, and the milker inflations need to be changed. With a light step and a cheerful heart, I head out to the barn. Later, as we spoon in Mama's dinner of beef, mashed potatoes, and corn, Pappy clears his throat and fixes his penetrating eyes on me.

"I'm warning you. If you don't listen to your parents, you are going to regret it someday. There are certain principles in life that are important, and this liberal trend that Moorland Mennonite promotes is going to lead you down the wrong path. This talking you do to the preachers about us is just not right either. Gossip is condemned in the Bible. The Bible also says 'Pride goes before destruction and a haughty spirit before a fall.' You're way too proud for your own good."

A heavy weight descends on my spirit. The happiness that has been mine for these last few weeks melts away. I have not cried for a long time, but I cannot stop the flood that begins. I flee the table to what was once my room and let the sobs consume me.

I wish I had never come here to help. I don't care to talk to anyone. I just want to go somewhere far away. But I came here with the sole purpose of helping them so I stay and mechanically go through the routine for the next two days.

I look at myself in the mirror as I get ready to meet Gordon on this hot, sunny Fourth of July. I have dressed in a shirt and culottes. My knee-length, never-cut hair is neatly braided into a single braid that dangles down my back. My covering still lies on the dresser. I have never gone out into public before with my hair down. It has always been neatly wrapped around my head and covered from the eyes of the world. My head feels light, and I feel naked. It feels strange to be walking out the door this way, but I am resolute in my decision.

The head covering signifies a woman's acceptance of God's order of leadership in the church as defined in I Corinthians 11:1–16 (KJV).

> But I would have you know, that the head of every man is Christ; and the head of the woman is the man; and the head of Christ is God ... Every woman that prayeth or prophesieth with her head uncovered dishonoureth her head: for that is even all one as if she were shaven. For if the woman be not covered, let her also be shorn ... For a man indeed ought not to cover his head, forasmuch as he is the image and glory of God: but the woman is the glory of man.

Not wearing the covering is a huge transgression against the beliefs of the Mennonite church, worthy of discipline. It is not that I have anything in particular against this symbol of submission to God, but I have decided that it is time to break away from the stigma of my family in this close-knit community. It is time to embrace the only chance I have of ever beginning my own family. Because I strongly believe that members should keep their promises to be faithful to the rules of the church, I have written a letter to the bishop of the Mennonite church, asking that my membership be withdrawn.

Gordon and I continue to date throughout the summer. By the end of September, I know it is time to tell the folks. I drive home on a Saturday in late September. Mama always seems like a safer bet to share any news with than Pappy. I approach her in the dining room after lunch. The house is quiet as Pappy and Paul are out in the field occupied with bringing in another harvest. Mama sits on the couch reading the *Budget*, an Amish-Mennonite newspaper.

"Mama, I am dating someone. Just thought you might like to know. By the way, he is Lutheran."

She looks up at me quizzically with those brown eyes embedded in a little round face. Her brow creases into furrows.

"Well, you had better stop seeing him before you have to marry him," are the first words out of her mouth.

That went well. She obviously has no faith in me. But what did I expect?

"I would like to bring him next Sunday for lunch so you can meet him," I continue.

"I guess that would be okay," she finally agrees.

The next Sunday, Gordon and I visit the Covenant Church in Superior for the worship service. We hastily exit the sanctuary as soon as the service is over. I figure about an hour should get us to the farm. We should be there no later than 12:30 p.m. My stomach has tied into its familiar knot by the time we park outside the house. I walk ahead of Gordon into the mudroom, on through the kitchen, and into the dining room. I stop. I am not sure whether I should laugh or cry. I am embarrassed for Gordon. Pappy and Mama are sitting at the table spooning in their food. Paul has already eaten and gone.

"You couldn't even wait a few minutes for us," I blurt.

"Well, we have things to do. We can't wait all day for you." Mama shrugs.

I can't quite believe this. My goal by now is to eat and get out of there as soon as possible. As Gordon and I drive home later, doubts swirl through my mind and discouragement descends on me. I was so hoping that Gordon would be pleasantly and politely acknowledged, at least, during this first introduction.

I hold a Bible in my hands as I slowly make my way down the aisle of the Evangelical Free Church in Superior to the organ serenade. The sun sends rays through the skylight onto the cross at the front of the church. I glance from the cross to my handsome groom in his gray tuxedo. He waits for me, smiling along with his brother and my brother, Joe, as his groomsmen. My eyes move further back for just a moment. Pappy and Mama are sitting in the second pew on the right side. Paul seems to be missing. I am not really surprised. I am supremely happy though. Gordon and I have come together on this September day in 1991 to say our wedding vows before God and these witnesses.

The past year has been full of firsts. Gordon proposed to me on Valentine's Day. I couldn't wait to say a resounding "yes." Then the whirlwind of wedding plans began. We decided on the Evangelical Free Church as a new beginning for both of us from a church fellowship standpoint. In the midst of sending invitations and buying the wedding gown, I graduated from the state university with my bachelor of science in nursing (BSN) degree in May. We also bought a house just outside of Algoma, the town where Gordon has his business, and I moved into the house on the first of July. Gordon will follow after we get back from our honeymoon.

Throughout all of our planning, Gordon and I try to decide what to do about Pappy and Mama. Mama has made it her mission to put pressure on Gordon to conform to their idea of how things should be. She wants him to become Mennonite. If he doesn't want to do that, she impresses on him that he should not be courting their daughter. She writes him a five-page letter in January and another letter at the end of February. Gordon finally sits down and writes his own letter to Pappy.

"I am asking for your permission to marry your daughter and for your blessing on our marriage. We both would really like to have you come to our wedding. But if you just can't find it in your heart to do so, we are going to get married anyway."

They did not respond to his letter, and we had no idea until today if they would actually show up for the wedding.

A year and a half has passed since our wedding day. Gordon and I have forged our life together. I still visit my folks on the farm about once a month to help with the calf record keeping and the bedding of hutches. Work is the only connection I have with my family of origin and the only thing they know. I reason that if I am going to have any ongoing relationship with them, I need to continue to assist in one fashion or another. I really do care about them and the struggles they face managing over a thousand acres and milking two hundred cows. I don't usually stay long enough to help milk anymore, however. A twisted knot is always present in my stomach when I am at the farm. When the day is over, I am only too relieved to retreat to my own peaceful home.

It is discouraging to realize too that nothing has changed on the farm. The hired help comes and goes. I can no longer keep track of the names of all those who have carried the label of hired man. There is never enough help. Today, I drive up the driveway and park in front of the house. I have come to visit for the day, but I have made a decision. I am not going to help any longer with any of the outside work. I have given them seven additional years of help every time that I can since my official leaving of the farm. I have always hoped that they would eventually see the need to change things so that they can handle the work without always needing to work 24/7. But I have come to realize that they have no intention of ever revamping the operation and that the struggle to keep hired help will be an ongoing one. Thus my guilt over leaving has lessened over the years and this final decision is prompted by a much more important pending event. I am five months pregnant. The baby is due in September.

Chapter 3

MORE TROUBLE DOWN
ON THE FARM

*E*rin, our daughter, is born in September of 1993. My life becomes centered on being a mother, a bookkeeper for my husband's business, and a nurse. But I don't seem to be able to walk completely away from the farm. I find myself driven by a force I can't identify to visit—to stay connected—about once a month for a couple of hours, though I no longer make any attempt to help with the farm work. Paul continues to rush around on the farm, moving from one project to another with nary a breath between them. He and Pappy, in a sense, farm together, but they do not plan their day or their seasons together. Disconnected—without a common goal—is the way that I would describe their partnership. By now, Paul is pushing forty years old. He has never married or worked or traveled off the farm except for short trips to church and to town occasionally. He has been dedicated to working the land.

By 1994, Joe has also been gone from the farm for seven years, most of this time living and working in Arkansas. While

in Arkansas, Joe had begun to date a young lady and the relationship had become more serious. When talk of marriage ensued,
the girl's father let it be known that if Joe wished to marry his
daughter, he would need to agree not to ever go into debt. The
man was concerned that Joe would become like his father—ob-
sessed with work and the need to pay off debt. Knowing that he
would always be prejudged by his father's behavior shocked and
angered him and turned his world upside down again. "It was like
having the mark of Cain stamped on me," he says. This knowledge
was the impetus for Joe to leave his job at the sawmill and return
home to the farm for eight months. He hoped that he had gained
enough distance and perspective to attempt a return to the farm
for a while. *Maybe this time things will be different.* His thought
process also included the idea that his helping would be his gift
to the folks for their fortieth wedding anniversary year. I think he
secretly also hopes that his return will result in his being accepted
as a son worthy of love and respect. And if things have changed,
maybe he will stay.

Joe and I have maintained fairly close contact over the
years. Now he relays an eyebrow-raising situation at the farm
to me. Pappy and Mama had hired a couple, Tom and Loretta,
several months previous to help with the farmwork. They were
good workers and together carried a significant amount of
the workload. Things went well for a few months, and then
Tom and Loretta separated, leaving Loretta, a small wisp of a
woman, on the farm. She lives in the trailer behind the grain
bins. Joe has begun to notice that often he can't find Paul when
he wants to ask him about something or needs his help with
some work. Where does he go? One day, following his intu-
ition, Joe knocks on Loretta's trailer door. Sure enough, Paul
comes to the door.

By the time harvest is over, Joe's mounting frustration leads him, at age thirty-six, to pack up his bags and move on again. Instead of returning to live in Arkansas, he signs up for six months of volunteer work at a Mennonite-run teacher education school in Ohio. Not only has he begun to realize that nothing has changed on the farm, but now he knows enough about what is normal that the "weirdness" at home just glares out at him. Also in spite of the fact that Pappy and Mama are seventy-one and seventy years old respectively, they refuse to leave the farm to travel or do anything else. Joe feels like his gift to them has been squandered. Only the farm matters, and Pappy still wants to make all the decisions.

I am not surprised either when a few months later Mama tells me that Loretta has been told to pack her bags and leave. Loretta being forced to leave is followed by strange behavior from Paul. He loses interest in the farmwork. He begins to write letters to the folks, long letters about missing out on the opportunity to marry and have a family, of never being able to experience the world, of having missed out on everything. He talks about leaving the farm and going to New York where Loretta has gone. He suggests that jumping off the top of the silo might be something he would like to do. Mama explains that Paul is "mentally unstable and doesn't know what he is saying."

Well, they said that about Joe too. This scenario sounds way too familiar. My perception is that Paul, at forty years of age, has finally awakened to what he is missing out on. He is in the midst of a midlife crisis. I am sure Pappy must be frantic. His last and most dedicated offspring is threatening to leave him with the farm. That would be the essence of total failure for a man who has done whatever it takes to "make a go of it." The farm, I have come to believe, is the symbol of Pappy's manhood; it symbolizes his success or failure in life. I believe Pappy is driven by a force that he himself does not recognize. His own father lost several farms

over the span of a couple decades, and I believe he is determined
not to be a failure like his father.

Although Joe and I are not aware of his actions for another
ten years, we believe that Pappy does the only thing a desperate
man in this situation can do. He promises Paul everything if he
will stay. In an analogy years later, Joe tells it like this.

"Our life was like a giant chess game. The king is the farm.
All the players can be positioned and moved around at will. If they
need to be knocked off the board, so be it—whatever it takes to
save the king and 'win' the game."

Though Paul has not acknowledged me for years now, I
still feel that I need to reach out to him. I know where he is
coming from. I have felt the same pain, and I would really like
to renew a relationship with him. I sit down and write him a
heartfelt letter. I want him to know that I identify with his
disillusionment.

"I wanted you to know I do not think you are out of your
mind for feeling taken advantage of and being angry. It brings
back many memories of myself ten years ago when I ran away
from home," I begin. I go on to encourage him not to put his
dreams and goals for life on hold until the folks are gone because "by that time the best part of your life will be gone and
the bitterness you feel will be hard to get rid of." I end the letter
by begging for his forgiveness for hurting him by "abandoning
him" and offer my support. "I wish to let you know I would be
willing to help you in any way I can if you should so need it or
want my help."

As I step out of the car at my next visit to the farm, I surmise
that Pappy and Mama are gone to town. That makes delivering
the letter simple for me. I walk toward the deafening roar of the
tractor. Paul, his long, lanky frame sprinkled with corn dust and
his face hidden behind a dust mask, is immersed in grinding feed

but glances my way as I approach. My heart thumps in my chest, and I hold my breath as I pull the letter out and hand it to him. He does not stop his work but takes the letter, turns, and walks away. I let out a sigh.

As the beginning of 1995 rolls around, my mind is turned away from the farm toward my own personal crisis. I had been experiencing some strange pulling sensations in my abdomen, which I shrugged off as probably just adhesions from the Cesarean section I had when Erin was born. Gordon, however, encourages me to see a doctor. I finally agree, as we are planning our second child and I want to make sure everything is okay before moving ahead with our plan.

"There is a large cyst on your ovary that we really need to check out" is the doctor's verdict. "It is probably not cancer, as you are too young for that, but we really need to make sure. We will do the surgery laparoscopically, and you will be home the same day."

Frightened but somewhat reassured, I enter the operating room a few days later. I know the instant that I wake up that it is cancer. There were not only a few small holes in my abdomen but a huge incision down the middle.

"It was cancer, wasn't it?" I whisper to Gordon.

He takes my hand, but his eyes wander away to the window for a few moments before answering. "Yes, the doctor called me from the operating room and asked me what to do. I didn't know what to say. He said he needed to take everything."

I feel like a ton of bricks has suddenly been dropped on me as the shock waves spread outward from my soul. I am devastated, not only by the ovarian cancer diagnosis, but by the loss of a chance to ever have another child. The doctor never talked to us beforehand about this possibility. With a shrug of his shoulders, the doctor dismisses my distress when I question him about the lack of preplanning. "You already have one child."

There are no visits from my side of the family during the week that I am in the hospital, but I have no one to blame but myself. I did not feel a need to tell my parents that I was going to have this "minor" surgery. Because of the diagnosis and its possible implications for the future, I decide I should share this life changer with my mother. I call her with the news.

"You don't really have cancer. I'm sure they made a mistake," she nonchalantly breezes over the information and on to the next topic of their lives.

Her response leaves a hollow emptiness in my heart because the diagnosis does not feel like a mistake to me. It feels like a cruel joke. Here I am just a few years after getting married at age thirty-four, and any chance of adding another child to complete our family has been taken away. And my own mother brushes it off as if I have just made up the story to distract them from their all-important work.

I make up my mind to concentrate my focus on Erin, who is a busy one-and-a-half-year-old, to take my mind off of the terror of possibly leaving my baby motherless and the uncertainty of the three months of chemotherapy that follow. Though I am pronounced in remission at the end of my treatments, the fear that every pain I am experiencing is cancer will linger for many years.

Before this unexpected turn in our lives, Gordon and I had been discussing moving from the neighborhood that we were currently living in to a place in the country, but now we are not sure what to do. Do we want to venture into more debt and a bigger house with a potential death sentence hanging over my head? But worrying about all the "what-ifs" has never been my style. We decide together to move on with our lives, trusting that God will take care of us.

I begin to drive around the surrounding area, looking for a rundown building site that we might be able to purchase and build a new house upon. Because of county zoning restrictions, we can only build a new home in the country on less than forty acres if the land is a preexisting building site. However, one day, while driving down a gravel road, I notice a grove of trees in a secluded area. *That would be a great place to build a house. I wonder who owns it.* Upon returning home, I begin to search land records, looking for the name of the owner. It is listed in the county plat book as being owned by an insurance company. As I investigate further, I learn that this land is currently for sale. The owner had divided the one-hundred-sixty-acre section of land into four forty-acre plots for sale. Astonishingly, there is one forty-acre plot left, the one that includes the area I had targeted as a great place to build a house. Gordon and I are overwhelmed by this confirmation from God that we are to make this the next step in our life journey. We buy the land for a reasonable price.

The year, 1996, finds us moving to an apartment in town while we build our new house in the country. Gordon designs the house, acts as the general contractor, and does the electrical wiring. I take on the decorating. I love our beautiful home in the quiet country surroundings.

Paul has never acknowledged my letter, and I have been too wrapped up in my own life to be disturbed by that fact. However, one day in mid-1997, I pull the mail from my home mailbox and flip through it. One envelope draws my attention. I do not recognize the return address, and the lettering is handwritten. Curious, I tear it open and read. The letter is from a young lady who has been writing to Paul. Apparently, she obtained my address from Paul and his approval before writing to me. She tells me that she is a single mother of two boys and is looking for a man who has a Godly outlook on life. She states that she wants her boys to grow up in a Christian home and be able to live in the country. She tells me that she, herself, was raised across from a Mennonite family and that she has a desire to experience that kind of life. She shares her heart in telling me that she would like to have a laughing, happy family who generates "so much warmth in the house the windows steam up" and possesses so much love that it "seeps out the cracks." She signs off her letter by asking for my opinion and advice in regards to my brother.

I am caught off guard by the letter. Apparently, my communication to Paul must have had some impact on him. I can't imagine, for the life of me though, why my brother, who has pretty much shunned me and cut me out of his life, would tell any potential girlfriend to write to me. *What am I going to say? None of the things Renee wants in life are true of our family, and I don't see Paul being able emotionally to provide them for her. Does Paul even think about God in his rush to get from job to job? Paul's heart seems to be closed to everyone. Laughing and being happy as a family are not something he knows anything about either.* I spend a week thinking about how I am going to respond. *Should I just ignore the letter?* Avoiding situations has never been my way of handling things so I need to figure out a generic way to respond.

I care about Paul deeply in spite of what I think about his responses to life. I have no intention of sabotaging his chances at a relationship. I will suggest to Renee that she move closer so that she can get to know Paul better. I hope she will learn the truth for herself. Satisfied with my decision, I sit down to type.

Dear Renee:

I am writing in response to your letter about Paul. I feel like I am in somewhat of an awkward position here and "swimming in very murky waters." I have never been especially close to Paul, and I have lived away from home for about twelve years now, so I feel like there are a lot of things I do not know about Paul (i.e., thoughts, feelings, dreams), which makes it very difficult to tell you what you want to know ...

I guess the issue here is whether you and Paul are telling each other your expectations. Have you told him what you told me about wanting a Godly man, lots of children, and plenty of affection? How does he respond to your dreams?

From my viewpoint, I do not feel we grew up in a house where there was so much warmth and happiness the "windows steamed up" so that part of your dream concerns me.

I don't know either what Paul has said about our father, but it will take two strong people together to counteract the strong control Dad has over Paul's life and the farm if Dad is planning on staying on the farm for any time yet. I am not saying our father is a bad man; he is just used to controlling the destiny of anyone under his influence. I have suggested to Paul that he should leave the farm for a while to establish an identity of his own, but I am not sure he can emotionally do that in that he feels he will lose everything he has worked for all these years ...

My most strongly felt suggestion to you would be if you both get to the point that you are serious at all,

I would suggest that one of you make a move. Either you move closer to Paul and work on the farm to see how you like it and how you relate, or maybe Paul could make a move your way and find a job there for a while. That, I guess, would be up to you two. I have always said you learn the most about what a man is like by observing him in his work environment.

Praying for both of you. Amanda

I read and reread the letter. *Have I raised sufficient red flags without throwing cold water on the whole thing?* Satisfied with my really-tell-nothing-about-Paul-specifically approach, I seal the letter and send it on its way back to Renee.

Gordon and my life as a young married couple continues with the usual activities required of our jobs and as parents. Our daughter, Erin, is a happy, busy four-year-old. The spring and summer of 1998 turns out to be a season of violent weather. We have several fierce thunderstorms that result in downed electrical wires in the community in June. This results in a busy schedule for Gordon, who as an electrician gets called into service when such things happen.

We, being outdoors people, do not take heed of the weather pattern of the past few weeks and reserve a camping spot for the weekend of June 26 in the county campground near Sun Prairie. This is located about thirty-five miles from where we currently live but holds pleasant memories for us of our dating days.

I drive the distance to the campground with Erin on Friday morning and set up our campsite so that we can have the spot of our choice. Then I drive home again. After Gordon is finished with work in the evening, we return to camp with two vehicles in case Gordon should have to leave on a service call. The evening is balmy and pleasant, and we sit around the campfire and roast marshmallows for s'mores. As the sky turns into the total darkness of night, the campfire is extinguished and we snuggle into our sleeping bags.

"Attention! Attention!" blares the loudspeaker from the camp headquarters building. "A tornado warning has been issued. A tornado is headed toward the campground. Take shelter immediately."

Gordon and I scramble for the flashlights. Erin begins to cry, "I want to go home."

We need to quickly make a decision as to what to do. We desert our sleeping bags and hastily pull on clothes. Our adrenaline-spiked brains push us toward speeding for home thirty-five miles away. We throw our food, the frantic child, and the dog into the car and set out, going north on the county road toward the next small town, each in our own vehicle. My heart is palpitating, and fear grips me as I listen to the radio announcer warn that a tornado is headed right toward the town we are driving into. The rain has begun plastering down in sheets, and lightning rips the sky. Do we stop? Do we keep on driving? I have no idea what the safe thing to do is. I certainly don't relish lying in a ditch with a dog and a four-year-old. I don't see any tornado during the flashes that light the sky so I keep driving east toward home, hoping that this will take us away from the storm area. Driving gets more and more difficult as we approach Algoma, where Gordon's shop is located, and we decide to take refuge there until the wind and the rain let up. Finally, around midnight, we drive the last six miles home and bed down in the basement.

The next day, Saturday, dawns bright and sunny. Gordon and

I decide to return to the campground to continue our camping adventure, and we are going to stay no matter what. *After all, it won't storm two nights in a row.* We have a great day hiking the trails and observing the animals in the small zoo at the park. As we sit around the campfire again Saturday evening, we are visited by the park ranger.

"There are storms headed this way. There is a tornado watch for tonight."

Now what should we do? Is it time to give up this attempt at camping? We hurriedly pack our tent and camping supplies into the vehicles. By the time we are done, it has started to rain. The sky grows darker and darker behind us as we make the run for home again. The wind begins its howl, and the driving rain begins again. All speed limits are ignored as we race for the garage. As the garage door hits the floor behind us, we are thrown into pitch darkness when the power is knocked out. We decide the only camping we will be doing is in the basement. Peeking out the basement window reveals trees bowing their heads to the ground as the water cascades from the sky.

Drip … drip … drip … drip soon reaches our ears. What's that noise? A flashlight-guided investigation upstairs reveals water running from the overhead kitchen light. The water is being driven against the house by the wind so hard that it is seeping through the siding and tracking through the light. As the wind and rain lessen, the phone begins to ring with message after message of downed power lines needing repair. There will be no sleep for Gordon.

In the light of day, we see that about a third of our twenty acres of trees has blown down, but the house is unscathed. Gordon works overtime for four to five days, helping to restore power to others. His generator is left with me as we have no power either for the next three days. This kind of camping adventure is a little too wild for me. It would be no wonder if our daughter never wants to camp again.

At the farm, Paul and Renee continue to write back and forth, but it isn't long before Paul finds his letters being opened by Mama and read.

"She's up to no good."

"She's not good enough for him."

"She just wants his money," is Mama's take on the situation.

It doesn't seem to matter that Paul is forty-two years old and it really is none of their business. Adding fuel to the fire, Renee comes to live in the trailer on the farm a few months later.

My soul is distressed by the energy that is marshaled into the crusade to drive Renee away, which begins almost immediately. I can only imagine that this will not have a happy ending. Saving the farm from the enemy, "that woman who just wants our money," becomes the goal of the folks. I often wonder, though, whether it is really Renee that they are opposed to. Or is she just the obvious individual who represents any woman that Paul might start a relationship with? I suspect that any outside woman would be a threat to the farm. Either way, in my opinion, Renee does not stand a chance.

"If they get married, I'm not going to the wedding," Mama informs me one day.

In spite of the hostility being sent their way, Paul and Renee set a wedding date for September 1998. But the next thing I hear is that Mama has called the ministers at Moorland Mennonite Church and cancelled the wedding. *Oh please! How does she get to have that kind of influence?* A new date in October is announced a couple of weeks later.

The wedding is held in the chapel of Millennium Bible School where the local congregation is meeting until they are able to build a church building of their own. It is a simple Mennonite wedding. Joe, as groomsman, stands beside Paul. Joe has been at home this fall helping with the harvest, making it convenient for him to participate in the wedding. Both men are dressed in the standard plain coat of Mennonite brethren. Renee, a dark-haired, tall, matronly woman, is attired in a beautiful pastel-pink cape dress. She has a friend as her maid of honor.

As my husband, our daughter, and I take our seat on the groom's side of the church, I notice that Pappy sits in the back alone. Mama is missing altogether. She really did carry out her threat to boycott the wedding. *This is ridiculous. How does she think boycotting the wedding is going to help anything? Letting the whole world know that she hates Renee is not going to get their daughter-in-law/mother-in-law relationship off on the right foot.* I am irritated as I snap family wedding pictures. *Apparently, getting a family picture is impossible for us. We never all get together any other time, and even at a most important life event, like a wedding, someone manages not to show up. In Gordon's and my wedding pictures, Paul is missing. This time, it's Mama.*

I stare at the wedding pictures once they come back from the developer. They are great pictures except for the fact that Mama is missing. Then, I have a bright idea. I take one of my personal wedding pictures with Mama in it and the best family picture from Paul's wedding to a film-processing place. I ask if they can take Mama out of my picture and put her into Paul and Renee's picture. They tell me that they can. A few weeks later, I pick up the doctored picture. I am impressed and pleased. One cannot even tell that Mama wasn't in the picture originally. For me, it is sort of a triumph over the dysfunction of our family. *Though I can't make everyone physically come to the events that mean something in our lives, I can make us look like one big happy family for a moment in time.* I print numerous copies of the picture and mail it to everyone in the family. *I wonder if anyone will notice the addition.*

Several weeks later, Renee expresses her feelings to me.

"I have been battling your mother's no-show at our wedding in my mind and heart ever since the day was here. She accomplished what I feel she intended to do, and that was to hurt me. It even pains me to see your wedding pictures with her looking so happy. And then she doesn't even show up for her own son's sake. I'm not sure I can find the Christian attitude in her decision. Did she think she had a hold on Paul so tightly that by not showing up he wouldn't go through with it? I'm not upset at you guys one bit about the picture. I really did find it humorous in the beginning, but as I let it sink in, she wasn't at our wedding! I'm sorry if I've said too much. I never wanted to say anything to you to put you in the middle."

"I'm sorry, Renee, that you are caught in the middle of this mess," I respond. "Just try not to take it too personally."

I know exactly what Renee is feeling, and my heart breaks for her. This is exactly why I knew I could not bring a spouse into the family farming operation. The environment there, without emotional and relational boundaries, is a marriage killer. As to being in the middle, I am already in the middle. Renee just doesn't realize it. I helped myself, I helped Joe, and now I feel a need to do what I can for Renee. There did not seem to be a backlash for helping Joe so I have begun to feel like I have regained a position of acceptance and some influence, an error in thinking that will set me up for major heartache later. I decide to try to talk to Pappy and Mama about how they are treating Renee.

"It doesn't matter if you think Renee is not good enough for Paul. She's his wife now, and you need to make an effort to live with each other."

"She's just after Paul's money. She'll stay just long enough to get it, and then she'll be gone. She doesn't help Paul at all ... She just sits in the house ... She's lazy ... Those children run all over with no supervision ..." The list of complaints goes on and on.

"Legally, Renee is entitled to Paul's money now. They're one flesh. It isn't helping anything to try to keep Renee out of any involvement with the farm." I try to advocate, but my words fall on deaf ears as usual.

Soon after this, Renee confides in me again.

"We are stuck here. Paul will never leave, and his dad knows this. Don't get me wrong. I love being on this farm very much, but not with all this turmoil. We don't get enough money to even feed a chicken. You wrote to me before when we started dating about it taking two strong people to get through this, and I am trying. I am also doing a lot of crying, praying, and pill popping for headaches all the time. I would really feel bad for Paul if we stuck around here all this time only to be screwed in the end. If Paul doesn't get this place as his heart is set on all these years just because your dad is mad at me, it will totally devastate him. And that part scares me! I really need your prayers."

"If it makes you feel any better, I have been where you are," I empathize. "The way you are being treated is not confined to you. I don't think it would have made any difference who Paul got involved with as far as the folks' acceptance. It is not a personal issue."

If I can only help her understand that the way she is being treated really has nothing to do with her personally, maybe she will be able to rise above the sting and not be hurt quite so much.

"I am here to listen whenever you need someone. I want to be your friend and a resource for you." I leave her with these parting words.

Why? Oh why do the folks feel this need to always keep things in an uproar? Why can't we just live in peace with each other? Stuck is too mild a word to describe the position Renee now finds herself in. I realize that she is now in the place that I was just a dozen years earlier. The sad part is that she has married into the dysfunction and her marriage to Paul has just begun. The only thing I can do is offer my support while trying at the same time to help Pappy and Mama see what they are doing.

Several years go by with little improvement in the situation on the farm. In Gordon, Erin, and my corner of the world, life moves along with a peaceful flow, like a meandering stream. The cancer scare fades into the background. Gordon's electrical business is booming, and I work at the hospital in intensive care two to three twelve-hour nights per week. This allows me to be home during the day with our growing daughter.

But every time I go to visit the farm, I am caught in the middle. The river of life is turbulent there, tumbling over the rocks like whitewater rapids. The tension is thick. My stomach is balled in a knot, and I dread every visit. I want to be friends with Renee, but my visits to the trailer are watched and scrutinized.

"What are you saying when you go over there? You had better not be telling her what happens over here. She just lies about us."

I hear all kinds of stories too about Renee from Mama. One day, I am told about a pushing match between Renee and Pappy. *I don't know whether I should believe all this nonsense or not.*

With every visit, there are more demeaning words slung about.

"She gets so angry; she looks like the devil."

"She locked herself in the bathroom and threatened to kill herself." They call the sheriff. "She's mentally ill ... She's bipolar … She makes no attempt to help Paul … She needs to learn to submit …"

In the midst of all this, two more children are born. Now there are four children and two adults living in cramped quarters in the trailer on the farm.

I try several times to talk to Pappy about moving off the farm and retiring.

"You need to get the farm positioned so that Paul will be able to take over when you are gone. Why don't you retire and do something else with the rest of your years? Take your portion of the money out that you feel you earned and let Paul farm the way he wants."

"I'm going to control this farm until I die," is his comeback to me. His shoulders are pulled back, and his eyes shine out their defiance.

Albert Einstein once said, "Insanity is doing the same thing over and over again but expecting a different result." *Is that why I feel like I'm spinning in a top? No one is willing to change anything so that things will be better.* I allow my shoulders to slump, and I look away from those eyes that I can never stare down.

"Can you at least switch houses then? Give Paul the big house and buy a nice trailer for yourself. Or let them build a house on the other end of the farm so there is some space between you guys."

Pappy just shakes his head back and forth. I slowly release my breath like a deflating balloon. I might just as well be talking to the wall.

But like any good daughter, I still long for my parents' love and acceptance. This keeps bringing me back to the farm over and over. And I still feel compelled to offer Christ's love to these people because they are my parents. I have always been taught that love is giving to the difficult as well as the lovable.

In 2001, I buy a computer for the folks and install the Quicken program. Mama has been doing the books by hand all these years. She can hardly write anymore. I want to show them how efficient a computerized system will make the task. Pappy tries to learn but struggles. Mama wants nothing to do with a computer. "I can do it just fine the way I have always done it."

I begin to spend my time when I come to visit once a month entering the farm and the folks' personal income and expenses into the computer. Now I have some specific task to do while at the house. It gives me a purpose for visiting and gives me some sense of being accepted there.

While visiting and working on the bookwork, I begin to hear much talk about stray voltage problems on the farm. The dairy has been struggling over the last few years because of cows that do not thrive. Many cows will freshen but then become progressively weaker until they are unable to get up. Finally, they die. There are always several down cows in various stages of dying strewn around the buildings. Paul and Pappy conclude, after consultation with various experts, that this problem is a result of stray electrical voltage. The solution, they are told, is to rewire the whole farm. And who could be more convenient to engage than my husband, the electrical contractor?

One of the things I love about Gordon is that he is a very generous man. So when Pappy calls in the summer of 2003 and asks for his electrical expertise, I am not surprised that Gordon agrees to help. I, however, have serious doubts about the wisdom of his doing so. I am worried that bringing the tensions of my family of origin into our home will destroy the peace and calm we have created for our family.

A new overhead service wire needs to be brought onto the farm. A new service and several new panels need to be installed and heavier wires pulled throughout the farm. The project is a

multi-thousand-dollar job if done for a regular customer. But
Pappy wants Gordon, as an electrical contractor, to buy the ma-
terials wholesale and sell them to him at cost. Because Pappy is
his father-in-law and Gordon does not want him upset at us, he
agrees to Pappy's request. Besides, it is not an unusual request.
Gordon has done this for other customers before. It is just that
this is a huge job and will impact our accounts heavily. Gordon
also feels that because Pappy is family, this project will be a labor
of love to my family of origin. This is how he has always treated
his family. The problem is that this generosity aligns perfectly
with Pappy's narcissistic approach toward life in general. Even
though he is getting everything at cost, he still scrutinizes each
bill to make sure we haven't charged him for something he hasn't
gotten. In fact, Pappy insists that we are not keeping our part of
the agreement because we bill him for gas for the one-hundred-
mile round trip each time Gordon travels to the farm. He expects
Gordon to drive there for free.

"I don't have tons of money to pay you. Electricians are way
too rich anyway."

Gordon spends many hours on Saturdays and some weekdays
throughout the summer and fall revising the electrical wiring at
the farm. I am becoming increasingly frustrated.

"Do we have to go to the farm to work again this Saturday?"
I ask one morning in late summer. "You're doing all this for them
for free, and they are not going to be appreciative anyway. When
are we going to have some time for us?"

"Paul asked me to come this week again, and Saturday is the
only day I have."

"But did you tell him we were going to spend the day going
to town and working in the garden?"

Gordon does not answer. I turn and walk away.

Gordon and I eventually begin to realize that if we are going to preserve our marriage that we cannot allow my parents' expectations to take precedence in our lives.

Throughout this year with our greater involvement at the farm, I have watched the raging battle between Renee and the folks. By now, I have begun to realize that this family cannot function without someone playing the role of the scapegoat. All the years that I was at home, Joe played that role. Now Renee has been assigned it. I am saddened. I am maddened. I feel like time is running out for positive changes to be made. Pappy is eighty years old. *Is he going to go to his grave leaving this legacy?* He claims to be a Christian. *Why can't he see what he has done to his family?* I decide to try to write him a letter laying out the truth as I see it and pleading with him for change. In December of 2003, I mail him the letter.

Dear Dad:

I have started to write a letter much like this several times over the years and have always put my pen away believing that my heart would not be heard anyway. My burden has been brought to the forefront again by our conversation last week about Renee. I ask you to hear with your heart for just a few moments and think about what I have to say without trying to come up with a defense.

I feel much sadness at the poor relationships within our family and grief over the loss of a relationship that I haven't known for quite some time … I long for a father who is vulnerable, has longings and defeats, and is open to letting others fail and make choices even if he doesn't think they are right without condemning them.

As a child, I remember a father who took great interest in his children. I loved riding with you on the tractor and in the truck to get shavings every week. I loved working alongside you, and my greatest desire in life was to please you and make you proud of me. I felt loved, cared for, and of value. As I grew into my teen years, I felt I could talk to you and tell you my heart and you would listen. I learned to work hard, to stick to what I started, to not give up, to manage money well, and most of all I learned about a relationship with Jesus.

But as we grew into our late teens, I sensed a distinct change in your attitude … Even though we were now young adults, our input was no longer sought in decisions, and decisions about the farm and its operation were made only on the basis of what you wanted to do … I know you feel you had to do those type of things to "make things work out." But I'm really confused by that. Have things worked out? Are you truly happy and at peace with how your life has turned out?

Paul, Joe, and I were all frustrated, and I became angrier as time went by as you tried more and more to control every aspect of daily life from when the parlor door was shut to when I bedded hutches to when Joe scraped stalls. These were details of our lives that I am sure could have been negotiated and compromised on. I felt disrespected, unloved, unvalued, and trapped in a situation from which I could not escape and had no voice in. It angered me, especially when you quoted Bible verses to defend your position on various things that happened. I only wanted to be heard and understood, not preached at by a father who I never heard say, "I'm sorry, I was wrong ..."

... The result was that out of frustration, despair, and hopelessness I did and said things that were not in the least Christian ... The main reason I am telling you this now is that I see a distinct parallel in the way Renee acts ... Joe acted the same way when he was at home, and you also said he was "mentally unstable and irrational." Paul had a period of time much more recently where all the same feelings and irrational behavior came to the surface as well. All of them were dismissed as not valid. Don't you recognize a pattern here? No, it is not all your fault but it grieves me that you cannot acknowledge your part in it. Even if it's not your fault, you do hold the key to turning things around. I have asked myself many times as I try to make sense of things what crisis occurred when you were in your fifties that caused you to feel the need to tighten your control and make all the decisions. I came to feel that we did not matter to you except wherein we contributed to the farming enterprise. That attitude portrayal has carried over into all aspects of your life together with Paul's family. I know you feel you have the "right" to tell everyone how things should be done, but one has no actual power to make others (adults) do what one wants ... Everyone has needs, dreams, wants, desires, and to get along, all parties must be willing to sit down and put those needs on the table and be willing to negotiate for the betterment of all.

Don't you ever wonder what happened with your family? Doesn't it grieve you that there are hard feelings and poor relationships with those closest to you? Is this the way you want it to be left when you go home to your maker? My heart is heavy over the barriers that have been built and the children that are caught in the middle. I implore you to search your heart and hear my plea before it is too late. These things are said out of the love of my heart and not to condemn you. Your daughter. Amanda

I know that my letter is hard-hitting, but my experience has been that soft words bounce right off of my father. I feel like this is my last chance to penetrate the hardness. I pray that God will touch my father's heart with my words and cause him to turn in a different direction.

Pappy and Mama's fiftieth wedding anniversary is approaching in July. Even though I am struggling in my relationship with them, I still want to honor them for their long-term commitment to each other. I want to show them the love that any child who cares for his or her parent would. But how do I go about planning a special day for them by myself? I decide to contact the Moorland Mennonite Church and see if they will help me with a special surprise. They graciously agree to assist. The minister's wife lets everyone know that there will be a potluck after church one Sunday in July while I go shopping for a cake and buy some punch.

The day turns out to be beautiful and sunny. The cake is decorated with an image of their original wedding photo. And behind it is a poster board displaying pictures of various aspects of my parents' lives. Proudly exhibited are pictures of their children and grandchildren. Pappy and Mama are not expecting this day of honor and smile for the many pictures of the day. But there are no hugs or "Thank-yous" or "I love yous." I can only hope that I have touched their hearts in some way.

Ten months have gone by since I mailed my letter to Pappy. One day, while I am working on the bookkeeping in the office at the farm, Pappy turns his office chair toward me.

"I got your letter, but I didn't think it needed a response."

So why are you mentioning it then? I do not look at him or respond.

"I did the best that I could. I had no idea you were so unhappy. You just left because people kept telling you to leave because you weren't getting any money now."

My breath catches, and all my muscles tighten into taut bands. *How could he have not had any idea how unhappy I was?* I can never look my father in the eyes, but I feel compelled to respond to the computer screen.

"My unhappiness back then had nothing to do with money."

He continues his speech as if I have said nothing.

"My heart does not condemn me for anything that has happened or that I have done. I have not done anything wrong in my relationship with Paul and Renee. I am at peace with my God."

I renew my fixed concentration on the computer screen, and my fingers begin again their search for the keyboard. There is no point in acknowledging his words. I feel trapped in the same dynamic that has been present in our relationship for a long time. He is still the authority who does no wrong, and nothing I say will make a difference.

A couple of months after this one-sided conversation, I receive my letter back in the mail with a message scrawled on the outside in Mama's handwriting. "Dear Amanda," it says, "may this letter be placed at the foot of the cross and buried deeply. So we may all meet in Glory. To live happily together. With love, Dad & Mom."

What is this? The ultimate denial? A bunch of religiosity to justify it all? That same hopelessness that was never far away at home threatens to wrap its cloak around my shoulders even though I now live far away and in another world.

Renee, in desperation, finally approaches the ministers of the local Mennonite church and asks for help. Several counseling sessions are set up. The church makes basically the same suggestions that I have tried to make: put some distance between the families, begin to include Renee in the business affairs, and try to respect each other in a Christ-honoring manner. Pappy and Mama's response is "We haven't done anything wrong. These things aren't necessary. Renee just needs to settle down. She's just all mixed up in her mind."

The ministers at the church, also at their wits' ends with the constant criticisms being slung back and forth and the refusal of the folks to own any part of the problem, excommunicate Pappy and Mama from the church for "unwillingness to pursue reconciliation with Paul and Renee." Paul and Renee also stop going to church, but the chaos at home does not abate. I am saddened by this latest turn of events but so glad that I left the church years ago. There are no words to describe the shame that I feel that this is my family of origin. At least, I can shut out the irrationality and sad state of affairs by moving in a circle of life that does not touch theirs except when I choose for it to.

I struggle to open my eyes. I groan. I worked a night last night, and this is my sleep time. *It really irritates me when people ring the doorbell while I am trying to sleep.* I stumble down the stairs and pull open the front door. I freeze there in stunned silence. Pappy, dressed in his usual green cotton pants supported by suspenders over his gray shirt, is standing on the front porch. Nobody in my family except Joe ever comes to visit me. I stare at him for a few moments while my sleepy brain tries to make sense of this appearance. I recover from my shock enough to spit out an invitation.

"Come in."

I usher Pappy to a recliner in the living room and take a chair opposite him. In my half-asleep state, my thoughts race. *What could he want?*

"What can I do for you?" I finally ask as I scan his relaxed but unsmiling face.

"I came to tell you that I have changed the will. You can fight with your brother after I am dead and gone."

I shrug. I do not know how to respond. I don't know what was in the other will so it really has no meaning to me. He does not give me any other details, and I have no idea what he is talking about. *I'm not going to fight with my brother. We will work something out that is fair to all of us once you are out of the picture.*

"I am not going to let Renee get any part of the farm. She's only after Paul's money," he continues. "I thought about skipping my children altogether and just willing everything to the grandchildren."

"You do what you feel like you need to do," is all I can think of to say. I know enough about my father to know that he will do what he wants to do regardless of what I say. After his departure, I mull the strange visit over in my mind. I am confused. *What was that all about? Am I back in his good graces again?*

As I tell Gordon about the experience later that evening, I am resolute. "Remind me when the folks die that their money is not worth fighting over," I tell him.

I soon dismiss Pappy's visit as just another strange twist in our family saga.

Later that year in early September 2004, while visiting the folks, I learn that Paul's hand has become seriously infected from a minor farming injury. The doctor orders hospitalization for IV antibiotics. Paul refuses. Concerned about him and the situation there, I contact Renee the next day.

"I was just wondering how Paul is doing? Did he make the decision to go in and get his hand taken care of?" I inquire.

"Paul is not in the hospital," she replies. "We did go to the emergency room, but I could tell by what he was saying to the doctor, it was going to take a lot of convincing on the doctor's part to get your brother admitted for surgery."

I take a breath and blurt out my feelings of helplessness with the previous day's events. "I wanted to come over and talk to you yesterday before I left, but the atmosphere was a little volatile so I decided to make my getaway while the getting was good."

"I'm sorry if you got into the middle of anything over there," Renee responds. "Your dad spoke to me first and what he said and the tone of voice he used didn't set too well with me. I wasn't looking to be boss when Paul isn't here. I just wanted some space. If your dad was expecting some help out of the boys and I, I was not looking for him to be watching over our shoulders. We know how to do chores. We know how to chase cows. We know how to scrape stalls even though it isn't the 'scrubbing' method he spends his time doing, but the job gets done. All I was hoping for was to be left alone to do things we know how to do. He would just have to worry about things we don't know how to do or fix. I know how to do some things around here, and I'm not looking for a boss. I don't get paid here on the farm, and I wanted it that way for a reason. He is not my boss, and he is not my husband. It has been drilled into my head many, many, many times … this is not my farm. I have contemplated ways of living away from the farm. Those thoughts, feelings, and ideas have never left me yet. Your dad has told Paul and me to our face that if Paul lives off of the farm, he will sell the place. How do you like that for controlling?"

"So apparently nothing has changed since I left. Yes, our father likes to have total control," I concur. I understand exactly what Renee is saying.

Renee continues sharing her deep turmoil with the way things are, "Paul would like me to learn some things so when your parents pass away at least one of us will know what's what around here. But *nope* … Can't let Renee know anything. Gotta keep Renee in the dark about stuff. Renee is trying to take over the farm. Well, that's just fine. Then they can do the work themselves. Once they are ready to hand over the reins, I will accept willingly. But until then, the boys and I are not hired hands."

Silence reigns between us as she pauses. What does one say to the craziness and chaos that always reign at the farm? I want to be friends and to help, but I am essentially powerless.

"I suppose I have gotten enough off of my chest for now. I hope I haven't turned you away from me. I don't hate your parents, but they sure make it hard to love them. Thank you for listening."

The only thing I really can do at this point is listen. And I am comforted that Renee desires my friendship and is willing to share her hurts with me, even if I don't have any magical answers. My heart breaks for Renee and the position she finds herself in. I understand all too well how it feels to be trapped in a situation one has no control over. So Pappy is using his ultimate tool to manipulate and control them too—"If you don't stay here and do what I want, you'll not get the farm." If Pappy could just move toward an equal relationship for all the adults, farming together could actually be enjoyable. But he won't or he can't.

Chapter 4

THE POWER
CHANGES HANDS

*T*he phone is ringing as I step into the house after arriving home from a long day at anesthesia clinicals.

"Hello?"

"Dad had a stroke, and they took him to the hospital in Superior. Can you go and see if you can find out how he is doing?" Mama's voice is shaky.

Mama goes on to tell me that Pappy had driven to Superior this June day in 2005 to Fleet Farm. He had not returned home by late afternoon. Worried, she called the Fleet Farm store several times before one of the employees finally agreed to go out into the parking lot to check for him. There the employee found him unconscious, slumped over the steering wheel of the car. The temperature had climbed into the eighties during the day, and Pappy had been baking in the car for over four hours. Nevertheless, an ambulance was called and he was taken to the hospital emergency room.

My hands shake as I hang up the phone. I feel weak. I am

overwhelmed with my own life right now, as I am currently enrolled in a full-time training program to become a nurse anesthetist. I don't really want to deal with this, but since Mama doesn't drive any more, I get in the car and drive to the hospital. Pappy lies on the cart in a critical care bay of the ER. His eyes are open, and he groans occasionally, but he does not respond to anyone's voice. He is gray in color and wringing wet with beads of sweat. An overwhelming sadness comes over me. So this is how it is going to end.

"Do what you can for him," I tell the doctor. "But do not resuscitate him if his heart or breathing should stop."

I go outside and call Mama to update her on Pappy's condition. We have a short discussion about the gravity of his situation. Mama is calm and seemingly accepting. She soon moves on to the subject on her mind.

"Did you find the money?" she asks.

"What money?"

"Dad had ten thousand dollars in cash in the big wallet in the car. He was going to make a down payment on a trailer today."

"What are you talking about? There wasn't any money on him." I question her further.

"Then it must still be in the car," Mama insists. "Can you go out to the car and see if you can find it?"

I drive around the Fleet Farm parking lot looking for the tan 1982 Oldsmobile that Pappy drove. I do not know what I am going to do when I find it. I could not find any car keys in Pappy's possessions, and my call to the ambulance service has not left me with any indication of where the keys might be. I soon find the car, but all the doors are locked. *What am I going to do?* I call the police, but they tell me that they don't unlock cars anymore. My last resort is to call a locksmith. I lean on the car and think about this shocking turn of events while I wait the half an hour that it takes for the locksmith to arrive. *What is going to happen now? Is Pappy going to die or be a vegetable for years—leaving everything in limbo?*

Once the locksmith arrives, it takes him just a minute to release the latch on the driver's side door. There on the floor lie the keys where they must have dropped from Pappy's hand. Now to search for the lost treasure. I pull open the glove compartment door and peer inside. There it is—the big wallet. And still safely inside are stacks of greenbacks.

A couple of days later, I pull up outside the farmhouse.

"Here is the money." I hand the wallet off to Mama. "That's one wad of cash to be carrying around. You might want to put that in a safe place."

"Oh, we've always kept that here in case we run into an emergency," she responds.

I am dumbfounded. *I never even suspected that they kept such a stash of cash in the house.* I proceed with helping Mama into the car for the drive to the hospital to see Pappy.

Pappy slouches, propped and tied into a chair designed for folks such as he. His right arm lies useless. His mouth droops, and spit drools down his chin. His eyeglasses tilt to the right; the right bow hanging below his ear instead of in its rightful place. He tries to speak, but the words come out garbled. He doesn't seem so much like the hard-hearted Pappy anymore, and my heart softens. The man is still my father, and I transition back to referring to him as Dad.

Dad has improved some over the last few days, but he is left with some serious deficits. He seems to understand what is being said to him but is unable to speak anything intelligible. His right side is completely paralyzed. He chokes on any food that is fed to him. A decision needs to be made soon as to where he will go from the hospital, as he cannot go home in this condition without significant help. I push the staff to make arrangements for him to enter the onsite intensive rehabilitation program at the hospital. Regardless of what happens next, I suspect that Dad's reign as patriarch is over and a shift of power is about to occur. I, unfortunately, am completely oblivious to the fear and desperation that will drive Paul and Renee in the days and weeks ahead as control of their world shifts and threatens to tilt even further from their hands. I am mostly just sad that now there will never be a chance for a change of heart or of making things right.

One day, at the end of June, Renee contacts me to discuss the situation.

"How are you?" she begins.

"I am good. How are you guys doing?" I inquire back.

"I had a good talk with Joe and Marilynn last evening. But I must tell you I am kind of nervous about this whole situation. Your parents are not going to let go easily if at all. I don't want to be mean or anything, but I am leery about your mother trying to handle the financial/savings side of the farm. She is so vulnerable. She would probably sign any paper this 'Scott' guy would bring in front of her."

I nod my head. "I am also nervous about Mom making changes to lots of things by herself. She doesn't really seem to understand the implications of the changes Scott is making any more than what he tells her."

Renee continues, "I told Paul he better make himself available more when he sees cars around here. Yesterday, he was in the field and didn't even know the guy came. I came home from work and saw the guy's car, and my heart sank. I noticed Paul's tractor was gone, and I took off out the field drive to tell him he better get in here. What are we supposed to do? The only way to get your parents to turn things over is to try to take it from them. And I don't think that it is easy to get doctors to say they are incompetent either. Maybe your dad in his condition it could be done, but your mother is mobile and talking. I guess I need your opinion on where you stand on this situation. Maybe you three children should sit down with your mother alone and have a good heart-to-heart. Paul, the children, and I are at the mercy of two elderly people. Our lives are basically in their hands. And that scares me to death. Paul wants me to stand with him, but it all depends how messy it gets around here. Can you try to help? I know it is asking a lot of you, but I can't do or say anything."

"Renee," I respond, "I really do want to help you and Paul. I just do not know how much power or influence I have either. Mama still pays the bills and records all the income and receipts in her accounting book. I come and enter the data, but that is all."

I am in agreement with Renee's concerns and want to see Paul and her be able to assume control of the daily operations of the farm. I am also concerned that Mama seems to have become deeply involved with this Scott Renee talks about. Scott claims to be a financial planner/advisor whom the folks have worked with over the last couple of years. Mama tells me that the day after Dad had his stroke, she called Scott and asked him to help her with their finances. During this initial couple of weeks since the stroke, she has been moving assets around at an alarming rate at the direction of Scott. She cashes in some annuities and begins to move money from a money market account to a different money market account recommended by Scott in the company he represents. I try to talk to Mama about blindly following Scott's directives.

"Why are you listening to Scott instead of us?" I ask her one day. "It is making me very nervous that he is making huge changes in your investments all at once. This just doesn't seem right to me."

"Scott knows exactly what he is doing," she counters. "He drew up our last estate plan and will, and Dad told me to call Scott if anything ever happens to him."

I really need to sit down with Mama. We need to go over the finances and look at the legal papers they have so far to see just where things stand. My problem is that with being in school, I have no days to go down to the farm and investigate things.

By the middle of July, Dad has completed the rehabilitation program at the hospital. He has been moved to a nursing home nine miles from the farm for several more weeks of care and rehabilitation. I am surprised at the progress that he has made physically. I would not have ever predicted it from the lethargic state that I found him in that first day. He has gone from being wheelchair bound to slowly walking by himself with a cane. He has taught himself to eat with his left hand. He is determined to get back to the farm "to drive the tractor." But communication remains a problem. He can say "yes" and "no" to questions, but any attempt to form a string of words together comes out as gibberish. And because his right side is affected, he can no longer write. Sometimes, I am not even sure that the yes/no answers we get are connected to the question, so it remains a mystery to me as to how much he really does truly understand.

During all this, my concern that Mama does not truly understand the financial changes Scott is making continues. Mama seems determined to reject not only my advice but Paul's as well. As the days pass, small incidents poke red flags at my mind.

"Did you put the cash in the bank that I brought back to you?" I ask her one day while driving her home from a visit with Dad at the nursing home.

"I gave it to Scott. He put it in our bank account."

I raise my eyebrows. "And did you get a written receipt for the money you gave him?"

"No. I trust him."

"You trust him?" My voice rises. "You are making too many changes in a very short time. I do not really think you understand the implications of what you are doing. Are you positive that you can trust this guy?"

Something does not seem right, but I am not a financial advisor and she brushes off my concerns.

"He knows what he is doing. Just talk to him and he will tell you," she assures me.

I decide to do just that, and I send him an email.

> My understanding is that you are assisting my mother in making some financial changes in their personal finances as well as the legal arrangements with the farm. She also told me that I was to become the power of attorney for them if need be. I am very concerned for my mother at this time in her life, as she is very vulnerable and does not seem to remember what you are doing or why. This is leading to great anxiety for me and my brothers. I would like to make an appointment with you to look at the changes you are making and what you are proposing for them from a financial standpoint. I also need to know what legal responsibilities are mine and at what point they become mine. She says she has given you all their financial records so I personally cannot help her or advise her without seeing them. You may respond by email or give me a call in the evening. Amanda

Scott calls me the next evening. He seems friendly and talks freely about what he is doing. He has a logical-sounding explanation for all the changes he has made so far. He readily agrees that we need to set up a date to meet, but his calendar is full at the moment, he says. Though I have not been informed of the details of the latest trust that he apparently drew up in 2004, Scott alludes to some of the content without being specific. He assures me that he has no legal right to sign any checks and that everything that is being done is my mother's wishes. He goes on to explain how making these moves are in accordance with what Dad wished done. Everything sounds aboveboard. He is bonded and does work for a legitimate investment company. Furthermore, Mama does need someone to help her, but she is not totally incompetent so I really do not see any need to force myself into the transactions. I also know that I need to concentrate on my studies if I am going to make it through school. This latest in a series of family crises is not about to become my first priority. Though I still have some reservations about what Scott is doing, I basically have no concrete data to indicate that anything inappropriate is going on. I have always tried to give people the benefit of the doubt. Therefore, I push any nibbling doubts into the background. I further dismiss Paul and Renee's hostile reaction to Scott as an overreaction by them to one more person who is trying to control their lives and their futures.

In the midst of the financial changes, the conflict between Renee and Mama continues even with Dad out of the picture.

Mama complains to me one day, "The children are really getting on my nerves. They come in the house and tear everything apart when I am not here. Renee makes no attempt to stop them."

I have no reason not to believe Mama. The kids drive her crazy. But I don't understand why these two people can't make an attempt to get along. I have unsuccessfully tried many times to talk to the folks about how they treat Paul and Renee. Just maybe, if I let Renee know that the children are getting on Mama's nerves, she will be willing to make one small step toward peace from her part. After all, I have always believed that if one doesn't know that there is a problem, it can't be fixed. And facing the truth is the secret to being able to change the future. I truly believe, as well, that if everyone would be willing to focus on solutions that are workable for everyone, peace could be achieved. I am getting very weary of trying to be the voice of reason.

So after my talk with Scott Hanson, I decide to share the information I have found out from him and try to address the continuing tensions. I have always spoken the truth as I see it. I have never been one to beat around the bush. And I feel that Paul and Renee have been open to my opinions in the past so I decide to also share my slant on the situation.

"Hello, Renee," I begin. "I talked to Scott on the phone on Monday for quite some time. He seems to be on the up-and-up, but I guess time will tell. He was quite clear about the fact that no one has the authority to write checks or do anything legally with the finances of the trust and the farm except Mama and Dad. So I don't think there are going to be any changes at this point unless they willingly decide to remove themselves from the day-to-day operation. Once they are gone, Scott says Paul, Joe, and I must agree together what changes will be made. That is the way the trust is set up."

A strained silence follows my naive declaration, then a voice filled with anger responds. "Poor guy ... just because his parents didn't like his choice of a wife, he stands to lose the one thing he has worked all his life for. He planned to sit back someday, kick his feet up, and live off the rent of the farm. But now it looks like the poor guy is going to have to work at Fleet Farm or somewhere at fifty years old. So I suppose Joe knows this little bit of information about the trust too. But we just found out tonight. No respect for the guy who kept this farm going after you and Joe left. You and Joe signed off way back, but because your parents did not like

Paul's wife, they brought you guys back in when they wrote up the new trust. You know what ... I'm not surprised—hurt but not surprised one bit. My family and I have discussed this happening many, many times over the years. I actually warned Paul several years ago. But he just brushed it off and thought it would never happen. I have told him over and over that he better listen to me more, and here again ... I'm right."

I am stunned and taken aback by Renee's response to me. I did not expect this kind of a comeback at all. I do not understand the anger coming my way. I am simply telling them what Scott told me. That doesn't mean that I agree with it.

I try to explain my understanding to Renee, but I let my irritation with our inability as a family to solve problems reasonably and levelheadedly come through in my reply to her. "Scott says he was hired by Dad a couple of years ago and the things my mom are doing are in Paul's best interest in the long run. I don't know what the specifics are. I guess I am feeling the need to stay away again with all the hostility that oozes from everyone there. It seems like that once one has been in that environment there for so long, one loses the ability to be rational and it just becomes an emotional reaction. It happened to me, and I see it happening to you. I don't agree at all with the disrespect my folks show to you, Renee, but I really can't see any point in being unkind back either. You guys need to put some space between your families. I know my mom is particularly upset with the children coming in when she is gone and tearing the house apart. And they do. She isn't just making that up. Then she goes off on her threats to call the police, which are plumb ridiculous. I want to help you and Paul with improving things and making sure he gets to keep the farm, but trying to be a mediator is a thankless and unwanted job when both parties set their feet and hurl unkindness back and forth and are just plain mean to each other."

"If you feel I am not *rational*," Renee shoots back, "then how are Paul and I supposed to react when people off the farm are running the show and know more than the one person who was supposed to be inheriting this place? Nothing was ever discussed with Paul. So I guess thank you for your ... what do I say ... friendship? According to what you say, it doesn't feel right to say that anymore. Maybe ... nice knowing you? I suppose that used to be true. I guess all I can say then is good night."

I admit that getting in the middle between Mama and Renee over the children was a huge mistake, but I can't believe that Renee is ready to throw out what I thought was a good relationship between us just like that. But I suspect that my unsolicited advice is not the major issue. She is angry over what she perceives to be a betrayal of trust. She believes that Dad promised everything to Paul. Now I am telling her that all of us will be involved in making whatever decisions will be made in the future. Talk about shooting the messenger! I am not the one who changed the trusts. She is right that my father's reason for changing the trust (his own words to me) was to keep Renee from getting any part of the farm, but I still have no idea what either trust actually says. And I still believe that no matter what the trusts say, we can all come to a logical settlement that is fair to all once the folks die. If I am their power of attorney as Mama says, I should be able to work toward getting Paul his fair share. I believe, as does Renee, that this not leaving the farm to Paul is incredibly mean and unjustified. And I am not labeling her as irrational. I am simply trying to make the point that craziness begets craziness. I have seen this pattern over and over in our family. I am not condemning her either. I am simply trying to help her see what I see. I have lived where she lives, and it looks totally different from a distance. I am truly hurt by being labeled as the enemy. After all, I may see some things differently, but I am on their side. I have heard many times about farm families who become estranged over the farm, but I have never thought that this could happen to us.

Deep down, I find it very hard to believe that this is my family and I have prayed many times over the years for the healing of Christ to take place in the hearts of all those involved. My faith has been seriously damaged by the fact that my prayers have not been answered and it just seems that the hatred and hostility increase. I do not know what to do.

Three days after this exchange, I receive a letter in the mail with the return address of Mama. I rip open the envelope and pull out a letter addressed to Paul and Renee. A note in the upper left-hand corner says "copy please send one to Joe." *That's strange.*

Dear Paul and Renee:

Please! Don't be in such a rush to make serious decisions and lose everything that was worked hard for, including family. We need to go a day at a time. Ask God for His direction. Satan is busy. Keep the faith!

There are people out there that want to see us fail. But there are many good people that love us and want to help us. Our dreams have been shattered when Amanda and Joe left us. It was hard to get started here. They contributed a lot. After they left, Dad and I were determined to help Paul keep the farm.

When we bought the farm, I went to work at the hospital immediately. The word was around that the owner sold it and was hoping to get the farm back. With hard working together, we are still here. He was a mean man. We plan the farm to be Paul's to do as he sees as long as the outcome looks promising. The income is his, cattle, machinery, crops, etc. ...

Only if he (Paul) sells the farm, do Joe and Amanda receive the price of the farm. They should get something for their young years of labor on the farm.

We said very little about Renee to Amanda. Amanda makes things sound worse between us than it really is. (We understand why.)

May God bless her and forgive us all for our mis-understanding "gossip" by other people. We are still looking for what is best for you, Paul and Renee. We need to keep working together during these hard times. Like before. God Loves you. Dad and Mom

My eyebrows furrow as I try to take in the implications of my mother's letter. I am confused by her words. I have no idea what she is talking about with her comment about understanding why I make things sound worse between them than they really are. I see myself as only trying to help, so I am hurt by her comments about me. But I also find it interesting that in this attempt to pacify Paul and Renee, she says the thing that will most infuriate them and feed the fire of outrage—"Joe and Amanda receive the price of the farm."

Soon after the copied letter from Mama, I walk into their house for a visit. I have decided not to respond to Mama's stabs in her letter. I find Mama taking a nap. I decide to get started alone with entering the bookkeeping figures into the computer. I scour the desk for the farm accounting book. It is always kept there. I look under numerous other papers on Dad's desk, but I cannot find it. *Oh well. I will start with entering their personal checkbook entries.* I am just finishing up with these when Mama trundles into the room, her eyes still puffy with sleep.

"Where is the farm accounting book?" I ask. "I can't find it."

"Paul came and took it and all the bills. He said Renee is going to take care of things now. I wish he would bring it over so I can see what's happening and pay some of the bills that are due. They are just upset at Scott because they don't understand what he is trying to do. He's a good man. He comes by at least once a week to help me. He takes me to the nursing home to see Dad and picks up things I need."

I have always felt that the bookkeeping needed to be turned over to Paul and Renee, but I am a little irritated that they just took it away from Mama without her permission. She still has a right to know what is going on.

Another few weeks go by. Dad has maxed out on his Medicare allowed stay at the nursing home. He has made further improvement with mobility, but he still has many other problems. He is incontinent and is often wet. More significantly, he is still unable to communicate. The speech department receives approval through Medicare for a special seven-thousand-dollar computerized board that will talk. It can be programmed with specific short sentences, such as, "I need to go to the bathroom," "I'm hungry," and "I want to go to bed." It can also be used to type longer thoughts. The hope is that Dad can learn to use his left hand to type out what he wants to say. He loves to push the preprogrammed buttons to show everyone how it works, but he never is able to make the connections between his thoughts and the keyboard. He simply sits and looks at it when prompted to write down what he is thinking. I begin to realize that more brain damage has been done than previously thought, and now there is no question that he will not ever again be giving the orders around the farm. He is no longer a threat to anyone.

Dad comes home to live with Mama in the big house in late summer. He is dependent on others for most of his personal hygiene and needs help with dressing and eating. Mama tries to care for him, but she herself has difficulty getting around because of arthritis. She cannot comb her own hair because of a shoulder injury a couple of years earlier. Thus, a home-health-care aide is engaged to help. During the aide's weekly trip to the farm, she bathes both Dad and Mama, combs Mama's long hair, and shaves Dad.

I want to help, but I live fifty miles away and am immersed in anesthesia school full-time. Coming to help them myself is not practical at this time of my life. I need to stay focused if I am going to be able to pass boards. I still have a year and one half left of school. Then I hope to begin spending more time helping the folks with their lives. For now, it seems that Mama is on her own, though she can hardly move herself, to change Dad and care for him. I really think they need to get off the farm and move to an apartment at the nursing home where they can get help when they need it. Though Dad resists, Mama seems ready to make the move.

During the rest of 2005, Scott continues to come by every week to offer his assistance to the folks. Sometimes he takes them shopping, and sometimes he buys items for them and brings the items to the house. I am glad the folks have someone to help. I sure hope that he isn't just taking advantage of the situation as Paul and Renee believe. I call Mama one day on the telephone toward the end of the year.

"Do you want me to come and help make sure the bookwork is all up-to-date for taxes?" I ask.

"Oh. That's okay. You're busy with your life. Scott is taking care of it."

Scott seems overly kind and generous. My experience is that people don't usually do these kinds of things for nothing.

"Scott does all these things for you. How much are you paying him for his services?" I question one day.

"Oh. He just does it out of the goodness of his heart. He's the nicest man."

Another red flag waves in front of my eyes. "No one does this much for someone 'out of the goodness of his heart,'" I counter.

"You just don't understand. He's like a son to us and treats us like his mother and father."

As the calendar rolls into a new year, I am contacted by Scott.

"I need to talk to you in reference to your folks moving to an apartment at the assisted living center. I have found an apartment for them, but a decision needs to be made in the next few days or it will be gone," Scott explains.

I am all in favor of them moving to the nursing home apartment. They will definitely receive better care there. "Why don't you go ahead and secure the apartment?" I tell him.

When I talk to Mama, she seems happy about the move and is in agreement with our decision. Dad shakes his head back and forth every time the move is mentioned, but he really does not get to make this decision. It will definitely be safer for both Mama and Dad. And so in February 2006, Paul moves the folks to a small one-bedroom independent-living apartment at the same nursing home where Dad stayed for rehabilitation. This opens the way for Paul and Renee to move into the big farmhouse with their four children.

As time goes on, Mama confides to me that Scott is putting money away in an unknown investment account for them and each of us children. She doesn't know the name of the account, only Scott knows. "Scott is taking care of the money."

This, she explains, is so she can "hide" some of their assets from Paul.

"Paul keeps asking for money for the farm, and this is a way to keep it safe so we have some to live on in our old age," is her response when I question her more.

"Where are the statements for the accounts you have money invested in?" I ask her one day. "I don't ever see any statements."

"Scott picks them up and keeps them so that Paul doesn't know where the money is. I can't keep track of all this stuff myself anyway."

This seems rather odd to me. I am not really sure what to make of it since there is continued outright hostility between Scott and Paul and Renee. And the relationship is really not much better between Mama and Paul and Renee than it has ever been. Mama shows me one day where she has hidden the key to their lockbox.

"I don't want Paul to know where it is. I don't trust him."

All the copies of their papers are supposed to be in the lockbox at the bank.

Another concern is that I have never been able to actually get Scott to sit down with me and show me the documentation for where he is investing the money. The couple of times that I meet him at the folks' he always needs "to run." Mama does not seem concerned in the least. She is convinced that Scott is taking good care of them. He seems genuinely interested in making sure that the estate plan he drew up for them is carried out according to Dad's instructions. Scott has told me that "the instant one of your folks dies, I am coming to get you and we are going to the courthouse."

As we begin making plans for our family summer vacation in 2006, I decide to look into renting an RV and traveling east to visit Joe and his family.

After moving to the Mennonite teacher's training school in Ohio in 1994, Joe worked on a volunteer maintenance crew there for two years. During that time, Joe decided that he would not be

going back to Arkansas and sold his property there. The gentleman in charge of the maintenance crew invited Joe to accompany
him to the state of Virginia when his term was up at the school
in 1996. "I couldn't seem to put down roots anywhere," Joe says.
The next couple of years were a succession of moving from carpenter job to carpenter job with a few jobs milking cows thrown in
between. Finally, Joe continues, "I realized that if I was going to
make any serious money, I was going to have to have a consistent
job." Around 1998, he was offered a job hauling and setting up
storage buildings from Virginia to Pennsylvania, the job he still
holds today (2015).

In his own words, Joe chronicles his social life during this
time.

> I was also running with a single group and had made
> pretty good friends with a guy named "Marley." I
> learned to have fun with him and became acquainted
> with some of the girls he ran around with. We went to
> Chincoteague Island and rented a house there. Marilyn
> (my future wife) was along, but nothing clicked at that
> time. We also got a house in West Virginia once.
> Marilyn was head cook at the Mennonite Nursing
> Home. She didn't go with the singles much, but she
> was in charge of the lemonade cooler when there were
> carry-in dinners at church. I do remember once asking
> her if she was still "watering her father's camels" as
> she filled cups for everybody. She thought I was crazy.
>
> In time, I sent her a letter, got a favorable re-
> sponse, and we started dating.

Joe and Marilyn married in March of 2000. Gordon and
I were able to attend the wedding held in Maryland. Erin, our

seven-year-old daughter, served as one of the candle lighters. Joe continues his story.

> When we married, the opportunity came up to buy a small 900 square foot house in Virginia and I was able to pay cash for it with the exception of borrowing $10,000. Five years later by 2005, I had saved enough to double the size. Our daughter was born in 2002 and our son in 2005 in the midst of the expansion project.

Gordon and I have not been to visit Joe and his family since his wedding six years earlier. Normally, our family adventures are spent in campgrounds, on lakes, and in the wilderness areas of the western United States. I really have no desire to return to the east where I grew up. But this year, 2006, will be different. I begin to think too that it would be a nice gift to my folks to take them along on this trip. They have never done much traveling, and this will probably be the last opportunity that they will get to visit their son and Mama's brothers and sisters in the east before their death.

Mama brings along a big brown envelope on the trip. One day, while we are driving down the interstate, she pulls it out and asks me to read it. She tells me that I am to be their financial and health-care power of attorneys and that she wants Joe and me both to see their final estate plans. The trust that she has brought along is the one made in 2004 by Scott. I read through the pages. It is pretty much as Scott has been telling me. Paul is to get the farm machinery, the cattle, and all income from the farm. He is to be able to farm the farm rent free for as long as he desires. The farm, however, becomes the property of Joe and me on the death of our last parent. And only if the farm is sold do the proceeds get divided between the two of us. *No wonder Paul and Renee are not happy. No wonder Paul is pushing Mama to change the trust before it is too late.* But if I have the power of attorney, I am hopeful that I can affect the outcome so that Paul doesn't get cut out. I don't want the farm, and I am pretty sure Joe doesn't want it either. I just want enough for myself and Joe to compensate us for all the years we put in on the farm. Paul can have the rest. As I read further on through the power of attorney documents though, I realize that the documents do not list me as their power of attorney in either the health-care or financial arenas. Both documents list Paul first, followed by me, and then Joe.

"Mama, these documents do not list me as your power of attorney. If that is what you want, you need to change them."

"I'm sure that is what I told Scott. I'll talk to him when we get back, and he can fix it."

A few weeks after our return to Minnesota, I receive a revised health-care power of attorney. Paul's name has disappeared, and now my name appears twice on the document ahead of Joe's. *Interesting way to fix it.* I assume that since Dad can no longer sign his name, Scott simply took out page 4 of the document and replaced it with a new one. I'm not sure how legal that is. I never do receive a revised financial power of attorney, but I decide that I am not going to worry about it for now. I do not see any need to invoke a power of attorney as long as Mama is capable. I am willing to help her with the personal finances as needed. Paul has already taken over the farm finances. I just need to get done with school. Then I am going to get serious about reclaiming the responsibility for their personal finances and finding out what Scott is doing with their money.

The year passes as I return to my full-time studies in September while continuing to juggle being a mother and a business partner to my husband. Paul and Renee still believe that the farm funds are disappearing. The amount of money that they believe should be in the folks' accounts does not match the amount that Scott tells them is there. Renee calls me one day in November and again asks for my help. I feel powerless to help, as I am in the dark as well. And I am rather frustrated by the continual tension over everything at the farm. I find myself being rather unsympathetic to the whole situation. I don't see any evidence that Scott is taking the money. I believe he is just doing what he feels the folks want. *They're just unhappy about not being able to have access to all the money,* I conclude.

"No matter how much you feel the farm and the money is yours, the farm is still in their [the folks'] name and the plan apparently is for it to stay that way until they die. My gut feeling is that there is no way to make an ending to this that you will be happy with," I lecture them. "And unfortunately," I continue, "there is not a lot that I can do about the situation."

"If you are the power of attorney of your parents' finances, you should have been involved with the shuffling of the money from the beginning so that you would know what was done. Because now it is a mess," Renee responds. "Someone has to know what aspects of your parents' lives you will be in control of, meaning Paul feels it would be wrong for you to have control over the farm end of things. Make their medical decisions, do their personal bills/finances, supply their daily needs, but Paul does not feel you should have any part in the farm end. So somewhere there has to be a copy of this POA paper. Somewhere you had to sign a paper and get it notarized. Did you not read the paper before you signed? Your mother doesn't even know what kind of 'power' you have over them. Paul asked her, and she has *no* idea. Doesn't this kind of show you people that your mother's mind is getting a bit forgetful? Your mother should have a copy of this POA paper. It would be nice if someone would find out for your brother's peace of mind what kind of 'power' you will have … Just a bit of advice. You better find out what aspects the POA covers and then think twice about accepting the job. It might not all be peaches and cream."

Apparently, Renee thinks I have way more power than I actually do. I never signed any paper involving the "power of attorney" and feel helpless to try to obtain any information, as I have no copy of any POA. I am kind of confused as to what I actually can do at this point. Besides, my understanding is that a POA only takes effect if the person is incapacitated, which I don't believe Mama truly is, though there are some days when I wonder. She can't seem to remember from one week to the next where Scott told her that he put money or how much. I agree with Renee that Paul should manage the farm affairs. I would be more than happy to stick with taking care of their personal financial affairs and their medical needs. I just need to get done with school, and then I can try to help Mom more.

I stand straight and tall by my chair in my cap and gown, facing the podium along with twenty-five of my classmates. Today, March 17, 2007, is graduation day from the nurse anesthesia program. I got up early this morning and went to pick up Dad and Mama. They sit in the audience and watch the procession along with my immediate family. I want them to be proud of me and what I have accomplished in life as I walk across the stage to receive my master's degree in nurse anesthesia. I want them to know that even though I have not followed the path they thought I should that I am not a failure. I just need two more weeks to study for boards, and then I can focus on helping them with their lives instead of having Scott do it.

Chapter 5

THE CONSERVATOR

"Hello?" I answer the phone on this day in mid-June of 2007.

"I'm Dennis Miller from the Minnesota State Department of Commerce, Division of Insurance Fraud. I'm calling to let you know, as the daughter of Jay and Arlene Reimer, that they are the victims of fraud."

I stop breathing, and my heart sinks. He goes on to tell me that Paul and Renee, finally, on the advice of a lawyer, had gone to county social services and reported the folks as vulnerable adults. Paul and Renee additionally reported to the county that they believed Scott was financially taking advantage of Mom and Dad. This report triggered a police as well as a social services investigation. In the process of this investigation, it was discovered that Scott had been moving money into a so-called "Superb Generation Life Plans" account at the rate of twenty to thirty thousand dollars per month over the last couple of years. This amounted to a total diversion in the six-hundred to seven-hundred-thousand-dollar range. Conveniently, this account, they discovered, was his personal bank account, and there currently was little money in the account. He had proceeded to spend most of it.

"We met with your folks yesterday to inform them of our findings. We waited until we had confirmation of the allegations before talking to them. Your mother still doesn't quite believe us. She insists that Scott would never do such a thing. She also insists that they couldn't possibly have had that much money. Because of the amount of money involved, the court has placed both your mother and father under a conservatorship."

I hang up the phone in a state of shock. *Why would someone who works for an upstanding investment company choose to take advantage of two old people, especially when there have been two of the couple's children directly questioning his actions? I can't quite believe it either.* As I think about the situation, I begin to understand that he chose to take advantage not only of their age but also of the internal family conflicts and tensions that existed between us. Mama was "hiding" money from Paul, which was a good excuse for Scott to use to explain away the lack of statements from the investment company. The money Scott told Mama he was "putting away" securely for all of us was going into his little personal account with a fancy-sounding name. Mama trusted him completely and allowed him access to their farm and personal checkbooks and all of their investment monies. She trusted him above us, her own children. All of these elements allowed him to embezzle right under our noses.

A mixture of emotions spins through my head. I am angry that he betrayed all of us. I am embarrassed. I believed him and trusted him too. I feel like a fool for allowing myself to be taken in by his sweet, persuasive talk. I had so hoped that he was being kind just "out of the goodness of his heart" as Mama believed. *Why did I not heed the red flags? If I just hadn't been so busy, I could have followed up sooner.* Mama truly did need the help he was providing until I could get done with school. Now, it's too late.

I am concerned too about a conservator having been appointed. There is to be a hearing in July to decide if Patti, the current temporary conservator, will be appointed permanently. I am sure Paul will not be happy with an outsider managing their money because the farm still belongs to Mama and Dad. The farm and personal funds are all mingled together through an earlier farm trust into one pot. Consequently, a conservator would be managing his money as well as the folks'.

As the court-appointed lawyers have begun to look at all the legal arrangements, it has also been discovered that the last trust and will in the folks' possession, created in 2004 by Scott, is missing the signature on the trust and the farm was never moved into this trust. This leaves the last-known wishes of Dad, while he was still fully competent, to be of questionable legal value. Right or wrong, because of Dad's visit to me in 2004, I still believe that the provisions of this trust were the last wishes of my father. *Maybe now that this has come to light, we all have the opportunity to change what would have been a terrible outcome for Paul. Since Mama told me that I was to be their power of attorney, maybe we could just petition the court for me to be the conservator instead of Patti. Then I could be an advocate and supporter for Paul in all of our views that he deserves more than just the cows, machinery, and the right to farm the farm.*

In my naïveté, it never occurs to me that my motives will be questioned and that I will be seen as simply trying to finagle things so that I can get more. My only objective is to try to be fair to all and get for Paul what he deserves. I feel like I am the one in the best position to do that. I also make the unquestioned assumption that because I believe I am to eventually be the folks' financial power of attorney anyway, that Paul and Renee certainly won't have any problem with my taking over the conservatorship.

I talk to Paul on the phone about the issues the conservator appointment has raised. I present my proposal that we should all stick together and request that I replace the court-appointed conservator. Paul doesn't say either way that he would be okay with my being the conservator or that he doesn't want me to do it. He just keeps saying, "I was supposed to get the whole farm."

A few more weeks go by before the conservator court hearing. I am the first one there. I sit on the bench alone to wait. My stomach has tied into its familiar knot, and my heart is skipping beats. I have no idea what I am going to say if I am called to testify. Paul, attired in gray work pants and a buttoned green shirt, and Renee, dressed in a long flowing dress, along with two of their children, arrive. A baby was born in December, and since I rarely stop at the farm anymore, this is the first time that I have seen her. Their oldest son is to babysit while we are in court.

We all rise with the entrance of the judge. Dressed in his black robes, he is intimidating. How does one tell the truth in front of such a formidable figure? Do I even want to tell the truth and drag out all the dirty laundry of the family? My breath comes in fast, shallow inspirations. My muscles contract into tight bands, and I can feel the rising nausea.

The proceedings begin. "The court has filed with it (in regards to) these two matters, a petition requesting conservatorship for both Mr. and Mrs. Reimer ... We previously have had an appointment of an emergency conservator in two companion files."

Various people proceed to testify on the events leading up to the appointment of the emergency conservator. I listen quietly. There is no new information being presented here. The prosecutor does ask the social worker if either Mr. or Mrs. Reimer expressed to her any preference as to who they would prefer for a conservator.

"They have not," she replies. "They believe they can manage their own financial affairs. That's what they indicated to me."

The testimony continues with numerous questions of the temporary conservator as the court explores what information she has obtained and how she has conducted herself. She is finally excused, and Paul is called to testify. His serious face is ringed by a long, dark beard and topped by unruly thinning brown hair. I hold my breath as I sit perched on the edge of my seat.

"And your parents, the kind people that they are, really believed that Scott was helping them out, is that correct?" Mom's lawyer asks of Paul.

"He had a good story, and it looked like he was going to help in the beginning, but when statements didn't start coming and keep coming, then I began to get worried."

"Do you think that your parents need some help keeping all these finances straight?" is the next question.

"I think that they probably learned their lesson and that the family should be able to take care of them now."

"So you think they need a conservator?"

"The family can do it. They need someone to look after them and make sure that another Scott doesn't come around."

"And you would like that to be family?"

"Yes."

"And what do you mean by 'family'?" questions the judge.

"Well, there are only me as the main one and my sister under me."

The prosecutor then takes over the questioning of Paul.

"Well, when you expressed concern to your parents about Mr. Hanson within three weeks after they became connected with him through transactions, what was their response?"

"He's all right. He knows what he is doing."

"And how long did they continue to say that?"

"Until the Department of Commerce came knocking on the door."

"In the middle of June?"

"Yes."

"So how long were they not agreeing with you as far as Mr. Hanson was concerned?"

"From July of 2005 until June of this year."

"So why do you think it's going to be different now?"

"They learned their lesson, and there ain't no more money," Paul retorts.

"But hopefully, they are going to receive some money back from the investment company, and there will be more money."

"We are going to control it this time," is Paul's plan for the future.

"How are you going to do that?" the prosecutor presses on.

"Keep the checkbook."

"What if your mother says you are not going to keep the checkbook?"

I snort under my breath. Paul already has taken the checkbook away from Mama without her permission so there won't be any problem doing that.

"That's where I need to be appointed a conservator."

"So you think it is necessary to have a conservator then?"

"As long as I am appointed."

The prosecutor pushes on into a different vein. "So you are suggesting that you and your sister be appointed the conservator?"

"I would be the conservator, and if I needed help, I would watch over her under me."

That would be a real winner for me. I can be the underdog.

"So you think your parents do need a conservator appointed by the court?"

"They need a conservator that is in the family."

"The authority of the court is to appoint a conservator. If you have a conservator just by agreement or consent, the court is not involved."

"It has to be court appointed."

"So you do or do not believe that your parents need a court-appointed conservator?"

"If I am appointed conservator."

Dad's lawyer then is presented with the time to also ask questions of Paul.

"Is it fair to say your parents are not receiving any type of income from the farm?"

"Not required income."

"When was the last time your parents did receive income?"

"I suppose in the spring of 2006."

"What's the reason they aren't paid on it?"

"I don't know. I'm paying the mortgage, and I'm paying the taxes, and they haven't needed any money yet. The money that Scott took was supposed to take care of them because that all really was generated off the farm."

"So would it be your plan that your parents would start receiving income from the farm if you were appointed conservator?"

"If they need it."

"And specifically where would that come from?"

"The farm."

"In the form of rent? In the form of wages?"

"Probably just directly, just money."

"You indicate that you would not be opposed to having your sister involved, but you personally want to be in charge?"

"Yes."

"Why are you opposed to having a conservatorship with your sister?"

"Because of the attempt to try to reclaim the money."

"Would you clarify for me?"

"You have one person to deal with lawyers and trying to get the money that has been stolen."

"And you prefer that person to be you rather than your sister?"

"Yes."

"Why?"

"Because I know the whole ins and outs and the whole financial situation."

"Other than the thought that you know the situation better than your sister, any other concerns about having a co-conservatorship?"

"Not to my knowledge."

The lawyers then switch places, and Mama's lawyer has the opportunity to ask his questions of Paul.

"If you were appointed conservator, would you change your parents' living arrangement?"

"Not unless it's up to them."

"So you wouldn't move them out of their current lifestyle?"

"I wouldn't put them in a nursing home anyways."

"I'm sorry?"

"I wouldn't put them in a nursing home."

"Would you put them somewhere else?"

"I might move them back home if expenses get too high."

"'Back home' means in with you?"

"Replace a house trailer that was there already and put a bigger one there or something."

I hear my name called to testify. I don't know if I can do this. I raise my hand and swear to "tell the truth and nothing but the truth, so help me God." *But what is the truth? I really have no cold, hard facts, only a major alarm that is going off in my soul as to Paul's real intentions in wanting to be the sole conservator. If I express what*

I really believe, it will only further deteriorate a relationship that is
already strained.

I explain to the judge my feelings about Patti as the conservator and my wish for my parents to be treated with dignity and respect by a conservator.

"Anything else you wish to say? I didn't mean to cut you off," the judge encourages.

"I don't know if I should even address the conservatorship. My brother wishes to be the primary conservator. I guess I did agree to a conservatorship. I do not agree to him being the primary."

"Who would be the other conservator with him?"

"I would agree to, I and he doing it together. I would agree to that."

The prosecutor is eager to jump on my statements with her questions.

"Why wouldn't you agree to your brother being sole conservator?"

"I guess I have a concern about him being willing to finance my parents' needs as they grow older. You heard him say he will not pay for a nursing home, and I have said I can't take them home and take care of them. They are way too much work to take care of at home. They get home health care now. They can get better care if they need it where they are. I don't see him being able to do that, either, and the only reason he is doing that is so he doesn't have to pay for it."

"So in summary, you feel that the request that your parents have a conservatorship should be denied, but if it's not going to be denied, you and your brother should be put in as conservator with the powers?"

"I do."

The questioning continues, and the questioner switches again to Dad's lawyer.

"Other than the fact that your brother testified he would prefer to have the conservatorship simply because he thinks it would be easier to deal with attorneys, other than that, do you know of any other reason that you couldn't be co-conservators? Do you have any reason to believe that the two of you couldn't function as co-conservators?"

"Do I have reason to believe …? We are not always on the same page, but we could, hopefully, agree to work together. Obviously, he knows more about the farm, so I would let him primarily be managing the farm, and if he wants to pursue getting the money back, you know, I would be willing to sign for anything."

"So it would be your plan to take care of more of the personal bills and let him take care of more of the farm aspect?"

"Yes."

"Any reason you don't believe that this could work?"

"I feel it could work, you know, if we both work at it." *Do my doubts show in my manner?* I am being discreetly evasive too in the hopes of not offending my brother.

The questioning then turns back to the judge. My hands are shaking as he looks at me.

"Do you understand that there may be a lawsuit here that can be brought against not only Mr. Hanson but also his agency if there's been malfeasance or intentional fraud?"

"Yes, I understand that. I'm not totally opposed to a court-appointed conservator. It's just that my mom and dad would really like the family to be the conservator."

"Do you understand that there may be a perception of some inherent conflict that your brother might have in being the conservator, especially if income is going to come off the trust and the farm operation to the benefit of your parents, taking the position you have taken that he's going to try to save as much money as he can and maybe not give them the proper care that they need? I mean, those were your words."

My hands are clammy. I feel like I am trapped in an impossible situation. I can't say what I really want to say without causing a major uproar after I leave here. I feel a flush creep up my neck. I stutter. "Y-yes. I'm trying to say what I feel without being too ..." I stop. I don't know how to continue.

"I know," the judge encourages. "I'm more blunt. But he's not my brother either."

By now, I am totally flustered and have forgotten what he is asking. "I guess I do not totally understand what you are asking."

"Well, I'm trying to figure out what you are telling me. If you don't want to give a response to that particular question, that's fine."

I shake my head back and forth. There is no way to graciously say what I truly believe about my brother's motives.

The questioning goes on by other members of the team regarding details of how I have been involved in the finances in the past and what my intent is for the future. I am sweating by the time I return to my seat. Then it is Mama's turn.

"Ms. Reimer, the last time we were here, we discussed the money that you had given to Mr. Hanson," begins the prosecutor.

Mama does not wait for the question but responds immediately, "It was to hide. It was not for him to line his pockets."

"So when Ms. Hepner was appointed conservator, you didn't think that was a good idea?"

"I don't like people doing my business."

"But wasn't Scott doing your business?"

"Not our personal business."

"Scott didn't run any errands for you?"

"No."

"He didn't go in and get things you needed from the store?"

"We would pay him."

"You would pay him the costs?"

"We handled the bills."

A sense of disbelief flows through me. Mama just sat there and denied the true nature of the relationship between them and Scott. *Why? Because to admit it means that she really can't manage her own affairs?*

Mama goes on to detail how she believes Patti (the temporary conservator) has been withholding their mail unnecessarily, not allowing her to have the cash to buy groceries when she wants, and her general annoyance with what she perceives as treatment befitting only someone who is totally incompetent.

After hearing all the testimony, the judge makes his ruling. "I'm going to appoint the conservatorship under Patti for a period of ninety days, or three months, to see where we are at. At the end of the ninety days, I will review for a possible appointment of co-conservators as successors being family members; specifically, it would be Paul and Amanda."

I drive out to the farm after the hearing to talk to Paul and Renee. I want to see how they feel that the hearing went. I thought I restrained myself sufficiently not to cause a total volcanic eruption. I can live with sharing a conservatorship with Paul. As I step inside the house door, I am met by narrowed eyes emitting icy glares and set jaws. Renee turns her stiffened back to me and stomps from the room. I could not get a colder reception if they had packed the room with ice.

"There is no way that I am going to work with you." Paul's lip does an upward curl as he spits out his contempt. "I am not sharing any conservatorship with you." His long gray-streaked beard jerks up and down with each word.

I see. I try to carefully control my tone and to talk rationally about the hearing, but the hostility coming my way just about bowls me over. I soon make a hasty retreat. I am beginning to have second thoughts about even wanting to try to be a co-conservator with Paul. Maybe it would just be best if there was an impartial court-appointed person to defuse the tension and control everything. I am angry too that I am being treated like this. I have only wanted Paul to have what he deserves, and this is what I get.

I am sitting on the couch reading later that evening when the phone rings. The clipped voice and sharp words that assault my ear are those of Renee.

"Let's get this straight once and for all. You have no business being involved in managing the farm finances. You left a long time ago and gave up any right to any money from this farm. You did not keep your commitment so don't try to stick your nose in our affairs. The only reason you came home all the time over the years was so you could get more out of the farm."

I am stunned and shocked by her verbal attack and the flood of skewed beliefs. I would never have guessed that these convictions were behind the words that I have been hearing in the last few weeks. It had never occurred to me to keep coming home so that I could get more money. I only came home because I felt guilty about leaving them to struggle all alone and because I wanted to maintain some semblance of being a family.

I feel the heat rise up in my cheeks, and I allow myself to be sucked back into the craziness that I would have declared a few months earlier that I was no longer susceptible to.

"I don't care what you think," I snap back, "but I gave twelve years of my life to the farm. I am not about to say that I don't think I deserve anything out of it. I busted my butt for those people, and Dad told me he would see that I got something."

"We have neighbors, friends, and fellow businessmen who know how Mom and Dad set this all up for when they die," Renee counters. "And here at the end of their life, Dad still knows how he wants it all to end. Now since Dad is down and out, you want to walk all over him. You know how things were supposed to be. Joe knows how things were to be. You can't tell me you don't know."

I am furious, and I do not guard my tongue or my thoughts.

"I just don't understand you and Paul at all. I have spent many hours trying to figure out what the true wishes of my parents are. I am not ignoring Dad's wishes. You insinuate that I know what his wishes are—by your interpretation that means Paul should get everything the folks have—just because Dad now says 'yes' to all kinds of questions. I do distinctly remember what Dad's main wishes are and that was that you not get anything. He purposely changed the trust for a reason in spite of the fact that he can't seem to remember why now. You and he were worst enemies before his stroke. Now, he's your good friend because he can't throw his weight around anymore."

"So how much do you think you deserve?" she questions me.

I don't know. I haven't ever really thought about it. I throw out the first figure that pops into my head. "One hundred thousand dollars."

We continue our all-out verbal war for several more minutes before Renee hangs up. I am in an emotional uproar. *How dare she? Renee is the in-law. She has no business calling me up and throwing accusations my way that she knows nothing about.*

I back away from any further interaction with Paul and Renee. The realization dawns on me that I am perceived as a huge threat to what Paul sees as already his. Furthermore, I am deluding myself to think that I have regained any standing in this family. And it really hurts to have Renee accuse me of coming home and giving of myself all those years just so I could get more money.

But this exchange has triggered a cycle of family interaction that will repeat itself many times over in the months ahead, a cycle that I do not understand. Any communication or issues between

Paul and Renee and me will be passed on to Mama. She then will respond derogatorily. Mama's response only further increases my shock and humiliation when two weeks later, I receive a letter from her.

With our deepest love from our hearts to Amanda and Gordon.

Greetings in Jesus's name, our first love. What is happening …? Apparently you are bringing up the past. That should have been forgiven and forgotten. Under the blood of Christ. I remember several years ago, I found a letter you apparently wrote to Renee. Dad and I were disrespectful in training you. I kept it for a while then answered asking for your forgiveness and to bury all hard feelings at the foot of the cross.

By the talk we hear, you are opposing everything we are trying to do to settle things. You want $100,000 now from Paul. How is he supposed to farm? What do you need it for? What does Gordon think of your temper? It could upset your marriage relations if you aren't careful. Gordon seems to be a fine Christian who wouldn't take advantage of anybody. Keep The Faith Gordon. Get Behind Me Satan.

Also your profession needs to have clear thinking so as not to cause harm and death unnecessarily. You need to be relaxed. I am sure your daughter will notice your emotional upset.

All this bickering destroys any sleep at night. Hard feelings all around. Dad has always said Paul could have the farm when no one else wants it. You and Gordon seem to be doing well in plumbing and nursing. Joe and Marilyn seem to be satisfied. Happy ...

At your age, could you be experiencing some mental problems? Menopause late? Dad and I trust that you can find peace with your family. Do unto others as you would have them do unto you ...

Our prayers and love that God may bless you with peace and satisfaction. Your loving Dad & Mom

I stare at the letter in my hand. I don't think I could be any more traumatized and wounded if I had just been shot. The letter she talks about in her correspondence was the one I had written to Dad in 2003, imploring him to consider his ways. It was not written to Renee. *Was that little note on the outside when Mama sent it back to me, some kind of strange unrecognizable stab at asking for forgiveness? To me, it seemed more like a slap in the face.*

This whole conflict has gotten totally twisted. I did not demand $100,000 right now. "What do you need the money for?" she asks. *What does needing or not needing the money have to do with it?* I thought I was part of this family, and I gave twelve years of my life to the farm on a promise of pay later. She, herself, wrote right after Dad's stroke that Joe and I should get something for our hard work on the farm. Now she does a complete one-hundred-eighty-degree turn. I am totally confused, and my heart feels like a dagger has been stabbed into it. The tears begin to course down my cheeks. I cannot stop the sobs that begin to tear me and my beliefs about who I am in this family apart. My former belief that my mother cares for all of us equally as her children has begun to crumble in a heap of ruins around me. I just do not understand why she has turned totally against Joe and me.

A week later, Mama calls and acts like everything is just

fine between us. She goes on and on about how Patti is ruining everything.

"Just do what your brother wants," she implores. "We have to get rid of this conservator so Paul can operate the farm properly."

Soon, both Joe and I receive a phone call from Paul. Paul has never personally called us in the twenty-some years since we both left home. He tells me that he has been to see a lawyer, the same lawyer that developed a trust for the folks in 1995. The lawyer's advice to him was that we needed to all get on the same page and petition the court together if Paul is to be able to make any changes from here on out.

"I want you to sign a paper so I can get rid of Patti. Then, I can work on getting the trust developed as it should be. Mom and Pap can't do anything with a conservator in place."

"As it should be." *What is that supposed to mean?* I hear, "Help me get rid of Patti so I can go make a trust that leaves me everything." Mama and Dad aren't mentally capable of making a trust anymore, not one that is their own unbiased wishes. And I have no intention of providing Paul with the full unlimited freedom to make a trust that he just has the folks sign. My brother and his wife have just told me to my face that I have no right to any inheritance because I "didn't keep my commitment" and that Paul has "no intention of working with me." *And now I am supposed to just step right up and sign a paper that removes the only person who can prevent him from doing just whatever he wants.*

"No," I reply, "I am not signing any paper to help you get rid of the conservator. Mom and Dad really do need a conservator."

I talk to Joe on the phone later, and he indicates that he wants nothing to do with the process. "I knew when Pappy said it was 'my way or the highway' and I chose to walk away that I would never receive a penny, and getting involved is just going to bring back all those feelings of rejection for me," is his initial response.

I still believe in my heart, though, that if we really want to that we can come up with a solution that is of benefit to everyone. I am open to negotiating with my brother. I really do want the best for him. And so my heart swings me back toward trying again. I regret that I have said some things that I am sure were hurtful. I know that slinging accusations of greed at Paul and Renee is not helping. I decide to try again to reach out.

I stuff the turbulent emotions that churn within me and try to reason logically with my brother and his wife as I pen a carefully worded note to them.

> I am sorry, Paul and Renee, that I escalated the stress all of us are feeling by labeling your actions as greedy. I have no right to assign motive to your actions, and I think we would all be better off if we would agree to negotiate and work together to find a solution that is fair and equitable for all. I believe this can be a win-win situation for Mama, Dad, you, Joe, and me if we make an effort at it. To not do so is to allow a con-servator and the courts to run your lives, and it will result in significant loss of assets to the conservator. I think we can all agree on this.

Inwardly, I also agree wholeheartedly with everything Mr. Schmidt had to say about us needing to get on the same page and work together. However, there is more underlying this dis-agreement than a need for everyone to get onto the same page. I continue, "To me it's not about money. It's about being treated like I am not part of the family. I am more than willing to work with you guys if you will stop treating me like the enemy. But that is your choice and I will not step aside just because someone is screaming about how terrible I am."

The recorded phone message from Renee with her and Paul's own underlying foundational beliefs is not long in coming.

"We have a valid trust and wills. *We aren't changing the trust and wills.* By the sounds of it, you are the one wanting to change the trust and wills. All we are wanting to do at this time is to get rid of the conservator. You and Joe broke your commitment to be a part of the farm operation. You and Joe made the decision to leave. Like I said, Dad has told many people outside the family that I get the farm. There again, that doesn't mean you won't get anything. But you surely aren't helping the situation by being pushy."

A sense of resentment creeps into my core. I resent that Renee is speaking for Paul—that Paul allows his wife to be involved in a disagreement that should be confined to the three of us, who are from this family. And I am totally confused. The 2004 trust and will made by the folks with Scott did not leave the farm to Paul at all; I do not understand how she can say that they are not trying to change the trust and will. That's all I have been hearing over the last two years from Mama, that Paul keeps pushing to go to a lawyer and get the trust and wills changed. It would make sense to me that they would be trying to change it. I myself agree that it is not fair to Paul and is a complete betrayal of his loyalty. Is there another trust out there that they are claiming as valid? Are they claiming the 1995 one as the valid one? I personally have no idea what it says, but I was under the impression that the former trust was obsolete with the making of the one in 2004.

I have begun to understand that the fear of having wasted one's life that surely has been building for years while Paul, and later Renee, were under Dad's thumb has burst forth full force. I realize they have every intention of fighting for what they feel they deserve, which is everything. I ask myself again why I ever thought that we would behave differently than our father. Why did I think that we would be reasonable with each other when the time came? I am not going to waste my time fighting a battle I know I can't win. But neither am I going to make any effort to help Paul either. I understand that I am going to be made to pay the price forever for "abandoning them." I can't say that I hold any animosity toward them for being bitter and unforgiving, but if that's the way they feel about it, they're on their own.

It isn't long before Mama's caustic phone call comes. She accuses me of going to lawyers to try to get my way and of trying to work against everything that they are trying to do. I have no idea where she comes up with these strange accusations. *I have not been to any lawyer.* She accuses me of being greedy. *How does everything get so twisted? And why do Paul and Renee need to go running to Mama with every exchange?*

A couple of more weeks go by before I am contacted again by Richard Schmidt, the lawyer for my folks. Apparently realizing that Paul is not going to get a signature from Joe or me to get rid of the conservator just for the asking, Mr. Schmidt has come up with a solution that he feels will "resolve the issues among the children and ensure that Joe and Amanda would receive certain benefits from the estate and trusts created by Jay and Arlene, no matter what transpires with the farming operation between Paul and Jay and Arlene Reimer." He is proposing that an "agreement of heirs" be drawn up and signed by the three of us children in exchange for an affidavit to the court in which Joe and I join Paul in requesting the removal of the conservator. The "agreement of heirs" that he is proposing states that Joe and I are to received $200,000 each tax free at the death of our last parent and Paul is to receive the farm and any other assets. It sounds like an acceptable proposal. It is not an extravagant amount, considering Mama and Dad are worth in the range of six to eight million, but it is more than I need to compensate me for the years of work on the farm. When I question Mama about this arrangement, however, she seems evasive and noncommittal. "We just need you to sign a paper to get rid of Patti" is all she will say.

The more I think about this proposal and Mama's response, the more warning bells start clanging in my head. I am leery of any agreement made between just the three of us, as none of the assets are ours. From my perspective, I don't see how one can make an agreement regarding things that are not ours. To provide some validity to the agreement, I insist that Mama and Dad need to sign this too. But Mr. Schmidt explains that because my parents are under a conservatorship, anything they sign now would be null and void. Once the conservator is removed, though, they will be free to come back and add this agreement to their trust and will. That is the expectation.

"I am *totally confused*. Do I have 'stupid' written on my forehead?" I ask the lawyer. "I have been aware that Paul has been attempting to convince Mama to change the trust for at least the last year. I further believe there are no unbiased decisions made by my folks anymore. Dad really doesn't have a say in anything decision-wise anymore, and Mama goes along with whoever has the most persuasive power at the moment. I also realize Paul has the influence to get Mama to do pretty much what he wants so the removal of a conservator gives Paul free rein. Yes, I realize the agreement between all of us is supposed to take care of our concerns about who gets what, but all Paul has to do is convince the folks to sign something that reads differently. After all, it would be Mama and Dad's signatures and supposedly their wishes, and I'm sure in a court of law, their will would supersede any agreement their children made regarding their assets."

Maybe I am just being paranoid, but I am having a hard time shaking this conviction that Joe and I are just being used. This would be a wonderful agreement between rational people, but my family does not seem to be able to negotiate for the benefit of all.

But then a soft spot in my heart pushes me toward accepting the agreement. Just maybe this is what we need to put aside the past and to move forward together as a family. Maybe it will allow for healing and forgiveness. I want to do the Christ-honoring thing. I want to give it a chance. Joe is reluctant to even consider making any kind of agreement. "Don't hang a carrot in front of me to get my hopes up and then grab it away" is his attitude, but I implore him to go along with it so that we can lay the past to rest.

Since I am making a trip to town anyway to take Mama and Dad to the eye doctor, I decide to slip over to Mr. Schmidt's office while I am there. I want to discuss my concerns in person one more time before actually signing the document. The attorney, a middle-aged gentleman with a Santa Claus build, and I talk for several minutes, and he assures me again that our agreement of heirs is a valid legal document that will stand up in court. It doesn't matter if the folks make another trust and will after this because this agreement is between us children. He assures me that Paul can't get around it by taking the folks to another lawyer. Though I still have some reservations, I sign the papers and have them notarized before I leave. Additionally, Mr. Schmidt tells me that it is the 1995 trust and will that is valid and legal, and he will add this agreement to it after the conservator is removed.

"Can I have a copy of the 1995 trust?" I ask as I stand up to leave.

"Sure. I'll have my secretary photocopy one for you."

My heart pounds and my stomach churns as I rip open the thick envelope later that afternoon at home. I read each word carefully. I cannot believe what I am reading.

I intentionally omit all of my children from this my Last Will and Testament except for the provisions made for Paul Reimer as set forth herein. The omission of all of my children except for Paul Reimer is not occasioned by accident or mistake and is intention. My son, Paul Reimer, has stayed with us on the farm and we would not have been able to hold it together and have the type of assets we have today without his dedication and assistance. He is the one that should reap the benefit of his hard work ... All of my clothing, jewelry, ornaments, automobile or automobiles, books, household furniture and furnishings, and personal effects of every kind and nature used about my person or home at the time of my decease I hereby devise ... the same in equal shares to my son, Paul Reimer, and the issue of my son, Paul Reimer, by right of representation ...

Signed this 8th day of March 1995.

A blinding light flashes in my brain. *Now* I begin to understand the statements made by Paul and Renee. No wonder they are accusing me of trying to change the trust so I can get more money. Joe and I were literally not supposed to get one red cent for all our hard work by the decree of this trust. Now I understand too why Paul and Renee keep saying that they are not changing the will and the trust. Since it was discovered that the trust made by Scott was lacking one signature, they have latched on to the one trust that leaves them everything—not just the farm, everything down to the last book and dish in the house. They just want to make sure that it is properly completed. Part of completing it properly requires getting the farm transferred into it. It seems that Dad, for some unknown reason, moved the farm back to the original trust shortly after making the 1995 one. The problem with the original trust is that it does not provide for the distribution of assets.

I begin to understand too that Paul and Renee truly do believe that *everything* is rightfully theirs. I am stunned that not only is this their view, but for years, it was also the view of my parents. And none of them see anything wrong with this outcome. My world spins with this new knowledge, and I feel like the life's breath has been sucked out of me. Everything I have ever believed about being loved by my earthly parents has been shattered into a million tiny little pieces. I am worth nothing in their eyes. And if my parents didn't find me worthy enough to keep their promises, why would God? I was a fool to think that Dad would still choose to do the right thing simply because he promised.

A few days later, I call Mama on the phone and ask her why she and Dad chose to totally disinherit Joe and me in the 1995 trust. She doesn't even take a breath before answering, "Oh, the lawyers made it that way."

Nonchalant. Just like that. She acknowledges no responsibility. She expresses no remorse. She has dismissed my feelings as if she has just thrown me out with the trash and it's no big deal. My chest muscles tighten, and my breath comes in short, rapid bursts as tight bands wrap around my chest. I cannot believe this response.

"If that is the way you and Dad still feel about Joe and me, then I don't need to be a part of this family," I tell her.

"I'm sorry that you feel this way. You're making too big a deal over this."

Speechless and dumbfounded, I hang up the phone. My sense of disbelief at her callous, unfeeling attitude overwhelms me. I struggle with this expanded revelation. I can maybe understand my father's motive for what they did, but I cannot fathom why a mother would not stand up for fairness for all of her children. I am left confused, and any remaining endearment that I feel for this woman as my "Mama" is drowned in the depths of my rejection.

I see her, from here on forward, only as "Mom" out of respect for the life she gave me.

In the final analysis though, this document was made ten years previous, and I don't believe it was my father's final wishes. I comfort myself with the knowledge that we all have made a new agreement "with the intention of keeping harmony within the family … to resolve any issues relative to beneficiary designations of Jay Reimer and Arlene Reimer's estate or revocable trusts entered into by them during their lifetime; and to give certainty to the children as to what they can expect to receive as beneficiaries … and to avoid family differences in the future" (Agreement of Heirs, 2007). If this works, it will be worth it. I just want to be a normal family once.

Joe and I talk about this startling revelation, and in an effort to try to understand what happened, we look back over the time line, searching for the true reason. I was already married and had a child by 1995. Why would Dad choose to make a trust like this at this particular point in time? We both come to the same conclusion—that it must have been developed in response to the crisis with Paul. Dad's last son was threatening to leave, and the only way to save the farm was to promise him everything. It was the move of a desperate man.

I make a wide swing and pull into a parking space outside the apartment building at the nursing home where the folks live. I don't come here often anymore. I have pulled back from being involved in their lives since the reading of the 1995 trust. I find myself unable to give willingly to them anymore. I don't understand my mother most of the time. I made a comment to her a few weeks ago that Scott took advantage of the poor relationship between her and Renee to enable his embezzling, and she responded, "I never had a bad relationship with Renee. I was just trying to help her and smooth the way for her." Denial works for her, I guess, but it never resolves anything.

Nonetheless, Mom had some interesting news to share when I told her last evening that I was coming to visit today.

"Mr. Miller from the Department of Commerce and an IRS man are coming here tomorrow to update us on the issues with Scott. Paul and Renee will be here."

I didn't plan this, but I have never met Mr. Miller. I look forward to this opportunity to meet him and see what he has to say about the case and its status. Mom chatters away about the usual stuff. Right on time, I notice Paul and Renee pull up in their van. I slide the French patio door open for Renee.

"Hello," I greet her.

She does not look at me. Her jaw is firmly set, and her brow lines are pulled together. Without saying a word, she stalks right on through the apartment and out the other door into the general hallway. Paul follows her. I know exactly what has just happened. I am not wanted here. This is a deliberate slap in the face. A wave of intense pain and then anger sweeps over me. I do not say anything to Mom but sit in stunned silence. Paul returns a few moments later.

"We're going home."

Now I am really furious at the ridiculousness of the situation. These men are driving all the way from the cities for this meeting, and Paul and Renee are going to go home because I am there. I march out into the building's main dining hall to where my tall, thin brother with leftover farming stains on his clothes and tousled hair and unruly beard is standing.

"This is ridiculous that you act this way just because I am here," I throw at him.

He does not answer. I turn and continue my march out into the parking area. I pull open the van door and spit my rage at Renee.

"Get back in there and help your husband. I'm the one who is going home. I can't believe you guys act like this. I just wrote a nice affidavit for you so that you could get rid of the conservator, and this is the thanks I get for it. I try to reach out to you, and you spit in my face."

I slam the van door and drop into the seat of my car. I cannot see the road for the blur that covers my eyes and my world. I cannot stop the sobs that shake me as I drive the sixty miles home. *Lord, why does it always have to end this way?* I pray. *I try so hard to do the thing that would honor You, and this is how it always ends when my family is involved. Why don't You answer my prayers? I feel like You have deserted me.*

My child, He answers me, *I have taken care of you. You have a good career, a loving husband, a beautiful child, and a great church. You made the right choice to leave. There is more to life than money.* My sobs finally subside. I did make the right choice. I would never go back even if I knew I would get a part of the farm.

My husband, Gordon, has always struggled with dealing with the conflict in my family. He almost didn't marry me because of it, and I have purposely tried to keep him as far away and as uninvolved as possible. However, my emotions now are raw, and it has been hard to leave the turmoil at the farmhouse. I am consumed by the hurt and rejection of my family of origin and find myself focused on it. One evening while getting ready for bed, Gordon says to me, "You need to figure out how to deal with this, as it is beginning to affect our marriage and I don't know how much more I can take."

Terror strikes at my heart. I know that he is right. I do need to figure out how to deal with my broken heart, but now I have an added fear to deal with.

I force myself to attend a Freedom in Christ conference (Anderson 2004) that is being held at our church in October. One of the sessions of the conference focuses on forgiving those who have hurt you. The message is that forgiveness will set you free. But what really is forgiveness, I ask? The answer I receive is that it is "cancelling the debt" regardless of the other person's response. Every attendee is walked through saying the words for all those people who have offended them. Just saying the words, for me, does not fix anything. It all sounds so trite and simplistic.

Later, I take a few moments to search my own soul. I ask myself, *What is the debt owed to me in this mixed-up family situation?* In concrete terms, the debt is the money I am owed for all my years of work. But the money symbolizes something far greater than mere dollar bills. The money symbolizes my value or lack thereof to everyone in my family. It was impressed on all of us, over and over through the years, that our value was measured by how much we put into the farm. I really don't need the money. I can let that go. But how do I let go of my desire to be loved and accepted as part of the family, the debt that they owe to treat me as a daughter and sister?

The hearing regarding the removal of the conservator is fast approaching. I am torn as to whether I should attend. I really want to be there, but I am so hurt and angry over the events of the past three months that I don't think I can sit through another hearing without all my hurt and mistrust pouring out. I am just not sure what I would say if the judge asked me why I no longer wish to be involved and why the petition is for Paul alone to be conservator. I do not want to spill all my feelings to the court because that would prevent Paul from being conservator.

At the last hearing, the judge indicated he was leaning toward appointing Paul and me as co-conservators for the folks. Now my greatest fear is that he will do just that. Since Paul has made it very clear that he does not wish to work with me, I really don't want to work with him either. I just do not need this kind of turmoil and animosity in my life. Since learning about the contents of the 1995 trust, I no longer feel either that I have any value or standing in this family. I still have serious doubts about Paul being able to place the folks' personal needs and long-term care interests above those of maintaining the farm, but I now realize that the folks are responsible for this error in conscience. He has been indoctrinated to believe that everything is rightfully his. It would be a continual fight that I could not win. I am not even sure that I want to spend the time and emotional investment needed to protect Mom and Dad from this colossal catastrophe they have created. And so I make the decision not to attend the hearing. I am resigned to let what happens, happen. When I tell Mom my decision and why, she responds, "I'll just tell everyone that you are working."

In late November 2007, the court-appointed conservatorship is allowed to expire by the judge. Mom and Dad can now return to managing their own finances. Joe and I are left to see if our fears will come true.

Chapter 6

BETRAYAL

I open the door to two men dressed in black business suits. They introduce themselves. They are here from the investment company headquarters in New York to conduct an internal investigation into Scott's transactions and to decide if the folks will be reimbursed for their losses. It is March of 2008. There is still an ongoing criminal investigation being carried out by the State of Minnesota as well, but the investment company is moving ahead to resolve this claim as soon as possible. I answer the men's questions as best I can. One of the men asks me, "What do you think of Renee?"

I am not sure to whom he has been talking, but I sidestep the question. "She is not any worse than anyone else," I say.

I have no interest in dragging our conflicts into this meeting. I am simply here to help the folks get their money back.

A few weeks later, I pull an envelope from the mailbox. I recognize Renee's handwriting on the front. *That's interesting.* She has refused to communicate with me in any way since that day in October when she walked right past me at Mom and Dad's apartment. I have tried to send Paul, Renee, and the children gifts at

Christmastime and emails occasionally with information about the folks, but they are not acknowledged. I tear open the envelope and pull out two sheets of paper. They are revocations for any previous powers of attorney that the folks made in the past. *Well, Paul didn't waste any time in going to a different lawyer and establishing himself as the power of attorney.* I place them back in an envelope and mail them back to Renee. On a note, I write, "We are not going to act like this. We made an agreement to put the past behind us, and we are going to work together to care for the folks."

This same week in the established familiar family pattern, I also receive a letter from Mom.

> To Our Dearest Amanda,
>
> Greetings in Love in Jesus's Name. Last evening when I was trying to sleep, God revealed to me, if I had ever asked you, if you wondered what you thought was happening to your loved ones on the farm. After you piled your things in the car in ANGER to leave with no good-byes or anything. To go into hiding—to Darrel and Yolanda we heard later. Then come and take Joe away. At least he chose a better way.
>
> During this time is when the church decided there is disunity in our home. Long before Renee came. Whatever gossip was passed around all that time. So we could be excommunicated. Alvin (the minister) said, "It wasn't Renee."
>
> Paul said many times, if he knew you would break your commitment he would not have consented to come to MN. We did hire help for him. Dad worked harder. In the evenings, Paul would write letters of his thoughts, pouring out his heart's miseries daily. That

was good because he was near or in a nervous break-
down. Daddy worked side by side with him and both
told him we wanted him to have the farm. Otherwise,
we would lose all.

After all, you have two businesses, electric and
nursing. Why be jealous of what he is trying to do?
His heart is in farming and it isn't easy to keep ahead
of debt and income.

We need to trust in God to lead us. Keep the
faith—Get behind me, Satan! You have not been put
out of our family any time and we don't plan to. As
for me keeping business from you. I don't understand
so much of it anymore.

We need to go to Christ's shed blood to cover our
multitude of sins for forgiveness and forgetfulness.
We certainly want a united family in love to follow
the Lord. Live for Him till Christ returns. All our
love. Dad and Mom.

I stare at the letter in my hand. I cannot believe the blindness
and denial my mother hides behind. I have reached the point
where I am able to say that, at least, Paul and Renee's actions and
attitudes, though I don't see them as befitting a person who pro-
fesses to be a Christian, make logical sense. Having been oppressed
and controlled for years—living on a promise—they are not about
to let anyone take any of their prize from them. But I feel like I am
spinning in a vortex with my mother. Nothing she says makes any
sense. She changes her story and position to suit the moment in
time that she finds herself in. A sense of confusion and instability
threatens to overtake me. *Maybe I am the one who is truly crazy.*

July 8, 2008

"The defendant agrees to plead guilty to Count 1 of the Indictment which charges the defendant with mail fraud ... and Count 1 of an Information which charges the defendant with tax evasion ..." reads the plea agreement and sentencing stipulations of the United States District Court Case of *USA v. Scott Hanson*, filed in US District Court in Minneapolis, Minnesota.

The charges seem strangely removed from the actual crime of embezzling and stealing funds. But apparently, one can receive a longer sentence for tax evasion and mail fraud than for stealing from old people so Scott has been charged with not reporting to the IRS as taxable income all that money he took. I suppose that works since Scott's defense is that Mom gave him that money of her own free will.

Throughout the last few months, I have tried to ignore Paul and Renee's animosity and continued to reach out to them. I have gained access to a federal court website where I can obtain copies of the documents that have been filed in the case. I have sent some of them by email to Paul and Renee. I decide to stop at the farm one day when I go to visit the folks. I have a whole pack of court papers I think they might like to have. I see Renee working in the yard as I drive up. Surprise registers in her eyes when she turns toward me. It is obvious that she did not expect to see me. We chat about horses and farm stuff for a few minutes. Paul strolls up.

"What do you want?"

"I brought some court papers I got off the Internet that I thought you might like to read." I hand him the papers.

He rifles through them and then tosses them on the ground.

"Nothing in there we haven't seen before," he grunts. He turns and strides away.

I feel like I have been slapped in the face, but I force myself to chat a while longer with Renee. She makes no attempt to pick up the papers. I decide I might just as well take them back home with me. My heart is heavy as I drive home. Forgiveness has to be a two-way street, or there is no relationship. *How am I supposed to make this better if the other parties won't respond?*

I know from things that Mom has said that they have settled with the investment company and that they have been working on updates for the trust with another lawyer. But she denies having any copies of their new trust and can't "remember" what the settlement with the investment company contained.

"All I know is that you and Joe get five thousand dollars per year," she tells me one day.

"Five thousand dollars per year! What kind of an insult is that? It would take forty years to get two hundred thousand."

She shrugs. "I don't know why you are so angry all the time. You'll have to ask Paul. I can't keep all this stuff straight."

"But we had an agreement that we all signed. Our verbal understanding was that you would add our agreement of heirs to the trust after the conservator was discharged," I counter her.

I can't believe that she is taking this position.

"I just wish you could see how important it is to everyone's relationship for you to stand up for Joe and me too, not just what Paul wants. You are enabling Paul to keep acting in ways that are detrimental to any reconciliation and peace in the family. If I am going to be able to continue to invest myself in your life and go to bat for you if need be, I need to know that I mean something to you and it needs to be in actions not just words."

"You're just making way too big a deal out of this. You're just greedy."

Her words cut, as always. I didn't think I was greedy, but how does one respond to such an accusation. *Does wanting payment for my years of work and then expecting everyone to uphold their end of our notarized document make me greedy?*

"Why didn't you go back to Mr. Schmidt like we agreed?" I ask her.

"He's a crook. He's just trying to get all the money out of us that he can."

I shake my head in confusion. I do not understand that statement. He got rid of the conservator for them. That was what they wanted.

I decide one day in August of 2008 to take Mom's advice and ask Paul for a copy of the new trust and estate plan. We have not communicated for some time, so I have no idea if I will receive any kind of response, but I feel like I need to try to resolve some of the issues if we are to have any kind of a relationship going forward into the future. I need the assurance that my fears of being used are unfounded. I want to lay the past to rest and build a new future. I still have this longing to be part of my family of origin, but I struggle with knowing how to fix the past. I was so hoping that the agreement of heirs that we made would be the ticket.

"Joe and I," I begin, "have both asked Mom for a copy of the new trust and estate plan that you are working on—or finished?—with an attorney, but she says I must talk to you because she doesn't really remember. I would also appreciate it if you would share with Joe and me what the final settlement with the investment company was and how you invested the money for the folks. We are both interested in hearing how things turned out."

I have apologized before to Paul, but it doesn't seem to have been accepted. I have carried this expectation all these years that Paul would be understanding of Joe and me in the end since he also had a time of disillusionment and almost left the farm. Just maybe if I own my part in this one more time, he will also be willing to own his.

"I want to say one more time that I truly am sorry for the pain my leaving the farm caused you twenty years ago. I know this has never been resolved in your heart, and at this point, all I can do is ask for your genuine forgiveness. Will you make that step of extending forgiveness to Joe and me for leaving you to struggle alone?" I implore my brother.

I can only hope that I am able to touch some guarded soft spot in their hearts. I cannot make Paul and Renee reconcile with me if they don't want to.

I continue my plea, "My hope was that the agreement we all made through Mr. Schmidt would help to outline what everyone expected and would help us all to move on toward forgiveness and reestablishing an open relationship. So I ask one last time, what is it you need from me in order to be willing to forgive and to stop treating me like I have no right to be a participating member of this family? I really would like to return to having a friendly, open relationship with my brother and his family. I would like to be a part of my nieces' and nephews' growing up years, but I can't make that happen without you. I am not going to come where I am not wanted."

I am actually surprised to receive a reply a few days later from Renee, but it does not offer the response that I had hoped for.

"Of course, as you know, I, Renee, will be typing this letter. But the thoughts are not my own. They are thoughts and feelings from both of us. Let me first say that Paul *is* letting go of the past. He says though '*just don't come back to turn the apple cart over.*'"

Astonishment and disbelief flood over me as I continue to read. There is nothing in Renee's letter that says, "I forgive you. Let's make a new start." It fairly screams "don't try to interfere with 'our' business," "you didn't keep your commitment" and "you both turned your back on EVERYTHING" are again thrown in my face. She avoids giving me any information about the trust or the investment company settlement, assuring me instead that "all the assets are within the cocoon of the trust." My brain feels like it has been stunned by multiple shocks from the cattle prod we used to use on the cows when they refused to cooperate. I do not understand how sharing information with me or Joe about our parents' situation can be harmful to their management of the farm.

I am distressed too that the statements that I made in the affidavit to the court so that Paul could potentially become the conservator are being used against Joe and me as proof that we are expecting something that we do not deserve.

"We have a copy of your affidavit you made during the conservator hearing," Renee has thrown at me. "You stated 'At the age of 28 in 1986, I made the decision to leave the farm. My father made it very clear that if I left he would make sure I did not get anything out of the farm. Joe left a year later with the same words echoing in his ears.' So for you to say that you don't know what Dad's wishes were, we don't believe you."

All that I really want from Paul is an acknowledgment that holding any teenager to some supposed life commitment is inappropriate. If we are to build a new relationship, I also need a commitment from him that he will honor our agreement and keep me informed of any major developments with the folks. I don't think that is asking too much.

"So the question," I respond, "still hasn't been answered by either of you. Can you put aside the anger and bitterness you have expressed toward me and move toward a relationship that is based on kindness and treating one another with respect? Sometimes people have to compromise and at least acknowledge that the other person has valid points in order for hard feelings to be put to rest. I am committed to putting away the harsh words of the past and replacing them with good thoughts if you are willing to do the same. I am committed to trying to understand your position if you are willing to try to understand mine. In the final analysis, this is about our relationship and how you want to approach the future, not about how I feel about Dad."

Mom struggles to get up from her recliner chair and then shuffles slowly toward their kitchen to eat the meal that has been brought by "Meals on Wheels."

"How are you today, Mrs. Reimer? Just a few more weeks and you won't be seeing me anymore," the delivery person greets her.

"I wish we weren't moving," Mom replies. "I can hardly get around, and I have someone to help me here with my hair and to bring us food."

Mom just informed me today that Paul has bought a new double-wide home using some of the proceeds gotten from the investment settlement and is in the process of making it handicapped accessible. Paul did not ask Mom if moving back to the farm was something she wanted to do. He has taken Dad out to the farm to see the trailer several times, but Dad, of course, has no capability of communicating anything to Mom. She found out about the plan from the home health care director at the nursing home. She was very upset.

"Why do we have to move? Everything is just fine here."

"Well, then just tell him that you are not moving," I advise her.

"Oh well, Dad wants to move so I guess we will just have to

do it. We can fall out there and break our hips as well as here," is her backpedaling response. That's my mother—never able to stand up for herself or anything that is right.

"Why are you letting Dad make a decision that you know is not a safe one for either of you? Dad is not capable of understanding the implications of this. You move out there, and you are going to be stuck," I plead with her.

"We just need to take it one day at a time," is her comeback. I call this "the cop-out," and it is royally frustrating. I have come to realize that this is her standard answer when she really doesn't want to continue a discussion, when the choices are too difficult.

"Maybe we'll die before we have to move."

I cannot help someone who will not help herself. A few weeks later, Paul shows up at their apartment door with the pickup and cattle trailer unannounced.

"Are you ready to go?"

And so they are moved back to the farm into a trailer. It irritates me that Joe and I were not included in this decision. Apparently, Joe and I are nobodies, undeserving of having any say in this family.

Soon after finding out about Paul's plan to move the folks back to the farm, I am contacted by Renee.

"I would like to discuss the letters and emails you have sent us—to try to help you understand some things," she begins. "Your parents said Scott's trust is junk. Paul actually read Scott's trust to them back in the beginning of the year, and they said it was not what their intentions were. They said they never read his trust before. They stated they never told Scott those things. Scott's trust was and is empty. So even if your parents passed away, their assets (including land) were not in Scott's trust. So in our eyes, Scott's trust is meaningless. The way we see it, all your efforts to 'be fair to all' were in vain. You didn't have to worry about what Scott's trust said and then try to make things fair for all involved. Nothing here on the farm changed regarding who was to get what."

A sense of incredulity flows over me. There are days like this when I wonder if I am just completely crazy. Did I make it up in my mind alone what I thought I knew? I seem to remember clearly the folks having a copy of this trust in their cabinet at the apartment and indicating to me that this was their last wishes. I know I was not imagining it that Mom brought it along on our trip to Virginia so that Joe and I could see their last trust and will. And I also know I did not imagine Dad's coming to my house that day in 2004.

It has finally dawned on me that Paul and Renee know nothing about Dad's visit to me in 2004. I have never shared this with them. They have convinced themselves that the 2004 trust has no validity, was made on Scott's own initiative, and cannot possibly be Dad's last wishes. Therefore, their conscience is assuaged and they feel justified in using the 1995 trust in which they inherit everything.

I challenge Renee. "According to you, Mom said they never read Scott's trust before. Is it a legal defense for anything that one signs to say, 'I didn't read it, and I didn't know what was in it?' Does that make it invalid? By the way, that is what our mother is also saying about the trust you are currently revising. Is that going to make it invalid too?"

"Your mother does know what is in the new trust. She just wants to avoid confrontation with you. But I think you already know that."

"And that is my whole point," I fire back. "She and Dad also knew what was in Scott's trust, and Dad did it intentionally.

Dad came to my house one day in 2004 after he made that trust and told me he had changed the trust and I could fight with my brother after he was dead and gone. I had no idea what he was talking about, but now I know."

Renee up until this point has been controlled and pleasant while presenting their explanations, confidently justifying their position. But now I realize I have hit the hot button. I have undermined their basic assumptions. Renee fairly screams at me, "Let me just say that you are chastising us for holding things back from you. But now you come along to say that back in 2004 your dad told you he changed the trust! You didn't think that would have a big impact on your brother's life? You didn't feel that would be something Paul should know about? What was your motive for not telling Paul back in 2004? If you wanted the best for your brother, why didn't you tell him back then? Regardless if you knew what your dad was totally talking about or not, you stated your dad told you he made Scott's trust and changed the trust. That statement seems self-explanatory to me. Why didn't you tell Paul?"

"Well, I didn't tell him because it never occurred to me that I should. After all, we did not ever talk to each other and I knew enough to know that Dad was going to do what he wanted to do regardless of what I said. Besides, I didn't know what the 1995 will said or how he had changed it so his statement really meant nothing to me."

Renee continues her outburst, "Another issue that needs to be put in the ground and buried is Schmidt's agreement. Here are some of our thoughts and feelings on that document. Paul agreed to one hundred thousand each. Schmidt made it two hundred thousand each. Schmidt said that that document must be put into the trust. So during the updating, the lawyer discussed this document with your parents. They were both asked what they wanted

to contribute to you and Joe. Your parents are the ones who set
the dollar amount to be given to you and Joe. So the document
was considered during updating."

Intense anger burns in my stomach, and an overwhelming
sense of betrayal engulfs me. Now Renee has hit my hot button.
She has just confirmed what I have suspected the whole time.
These people, who are supposed to be my family, are willing to
do whatever it takes to get where they want to go. They use us,
and just as willingly, they dump us with nary a twinge. I cannot
believe that my mother would do this to Joe and me. This is not
the mother I remember. The only conclusion I can come to is that
we mean nothing to her, only Paul matters. She has rejected us for
"shattering their dream." And she is willing to play dirty in order
to do it. It is a staggering thought and one that rocks my sense of
value in the world. I am no longer in reconciliation mode. I am
just plain angry, and I do not filter my reaction to Renee.

"The bottom line is that if Scott's trust had been completed
correctly and none of this had come to light before Dad's death,
Paul would have been sabotaged. Paul would not have inherited
the farm. So I would really appreciate it you would stop holding
it over my head that I have always known what Dad wanted to
happen. The whole point of saying any of this is that I wish you
could acknowledge that Dad manipulated and punished using
his money. I thought we were above acting like that, but I guess
that is not so. I guess I don't understand either why it is so hard
for you or Paul to at least acknowledge that the circumstances of
the past, first of all, occurred or that the behavior of our father
was neither fair nor loving. Is it because if you acknowledge it, it
might cost you something monetarily to do the right thing? And
about 'Schmidt's agreement,' it doesn't really matter legally what
Paul *says* he agreed to. He *signed* an agreement in which he agreed
to two hundred thousand dollars to each of us. Paul chose to sign

that document willingly. You are correct that the understanding was that you put that document in the trust. But you chose to not go back to Schmidt. You chose instead to go to a different lawyer to avoid doing _____. You fill in the blank. I don't know the answer. So my expectation is that Paul will execute his part of the agreement. If I had known he was going to stab me in the back, I would not have *ever, ever* helped him get rid of Patti, the conservator. I would have let you all just deal with her. It would have cost you thousands of dollars to pay her over the years not to mention the aggravation of her being in your business. So try to remember that you chose this route because it was supposed to heal family relationships and help us move on."

I am furious that these people, who are supposed to be my family and who profess to be Christians, can treat Joe and me this way. Do we not have any value to them at all? Do we not mean anything to them? I seem to remember a Bible verse that says, "It is better to not vow than to vow and not pay." Don't promise me something and then say it doesn't mean anything. Anger and deep pain overwhelm me. I want no part of this family. At this point, I don't even want to go to my parents' funerals when they die.

Chapter 7
TRYING TO UNDERSTAND

"Hello?" I answer the wailing phone on the wall. "This is Joe. What is this I hear from Mom? She says that you are taking them to court and suing them."

What is he talking about? "I have no idea what you are talking about. I'm not suing anyone. I haven't talked to any lawyers."

Then it dawns on me. Paul and Renee did the usual and ran over to Mom with our last exchange. Now everything has been twisted into a strange drama. It seems that nothing can remain between two parties in this family. Everyone has to get into the act, and it is always a little like playing "whispering down the lane." It is a pattern that seems to repeat itself every time something happens. I tell Joe about Renee's and my conversation.

"Joe, we made this agreement in good faith. I was so hopeful that it would allow us to chart a new course for the future. I felt it was the right thing to do, but now I wish I had just let the conservator stay in place."

"Doing the right thing is never wrong," is his response to me.

I hope he is right because right now, I feel just plain betrayed. I don't feel that I can ever trust Mom or Paul again.

A few days later, I pull an envelope with no return address from the mailbox. I know it is from Renee by the handwriting. Inside, I find most of the gift certificates for books that I have given their children over the last several years. All total, they are valued in the four-hundred-dollar range. Just because I told Renee that I expected Paul to keep his part of our agreement, she has thrown all of my gifts back in my face. Joe and I laugh sarcastically and declare, "This is the only inheritance we are going to get."

Joe and I split up the money. With my share, I buy books for Paul's children for their birthdays in the next year. That was the original intent of the money anyway. I know my relationship with Paul and Renee is over. This deliberate throwing of any kindness back in my face is uncalled for and beyond my ability to comprehend. I am devastated by their total rejection over an agreement that I thought we all subscribed to together. I comfort myself with the knowledge that there are consequences to all the choices that one makes. I know Paul and Renee (and unfortunately, their family too) will have a price to pay for keeping everyone else at arm's length and away from everything that he sees as his. The responsibility of caring for the folks until their final demise will be solely his. But the sad part of all this is that any connection with and support from extended family who really does care about them is being thrown away for nothing. In the final analysis, I never have wanted his farm and I release him to live his life there as he chooses.

But the hurt and rejection I feel from Mom is more difficult to brush off. The devastation and pain I feel at being totally disinherited haunts me. From my perspective, totally disinheriting one's child is the final revenge that reaches from beyond the grave and for which no recompense can ever be made. It indicates that forgiveness has never been granted to the offender for whatever offence is seen as worthy of such drastic actions. *Why have I never been forgiven? Why do they not love me? Do I not mean anything to any of them?*

Being used and betrayed again on top of the initial disinheritance twenty years earlier has only made the pain greater. I begin to fathom in a limited way the pain that Jesus must have felt when Judas betrayed him with a kiss. Being rejected by the world is one thing, but being rejected by those who should be your closest supporters is a totally different matter. I stop visiting the folks, and I stop calling Mom. I begin to search for books on relationships to help me in trying to come to terms with the pain I cannot let go of. I read fervently.

The books are filled with insights that I have previously missed in dealings with my mother. I begin to recognize that people who are manipulative use tactics designed to place the burden of blame, guilt, and unreasonableness on the other person. They justify their behavior by their "concern" for that person, and their desire is for that person to benefit from their intellectual superiority and frequently their religious insights. They are often unaware of their unfair maneuverings and shocked by what they consider to be the person's ingratitude and personal attacks on them. Wow, does that describe my mother! No wonder I feel crazy and have started to doubt my own motives.

Another concept that I discover that will become particularly useful in my situation is that of detachment. In order to stop the constant longing for what does not exist in a dysfunctional relationship, one must untangle from the emotions that swirl around and off of that relationship. In order to do that, one must separate emotionally from the person in order to work on oneself and to live one's own life. Detachment is releasing the other person to be responsible for him- or herself and to bear the responsibility for his or her own actions.

Realizing that this is something I must do, I make a purposeful decision to keep some distance between Mom and myself—to try to detach. But part of my upbringing keeps telling me that if I have forgiven her, I should willingly want to continue to help her. And to further complicate the matter, she keeps calling me and pretending that everything is just fine. Deep down, the part of me that needs my mother gets triggered every time she calls and the hope that I have tried to push down attempts to spring up again. People encourage me with, "It's never too late." But I cannot allow myself to believe that. It simply puts me in a position of being hurt over and over and over again. I feel torn because every time I get involved, I get hurt, and yet we are supposed to forgive "seventy times seven." I cannot reconcile in my mind how I can keep doing this. It is putting my life in a continual turmoil.

Joe and I try to move on with our lives, resigned that this is the way it is going to be. The court hearing for Scott's sentencing is coming up in mid-November of 2008. Mom asks me if I am going along to the hearing.

"No, I'm not going." I just don't care anymore how any of it turns out.

The day of sentencing turns out to be icy and cold. The hearing is in Minneapolis. Because of the distance and the road conditions, nobody from the family goes. Scott is sentenced to forty-six months in jail and two years' probation. In addition, he must make restitution to the company he worked for. I am more than happy to shut the book on that chapter of our lives.

One day in late November, I pull an official-looking envelope out of the mailbox. It is from a law firm in western Minnesota. I tear it open and pull out a letter addressed to Paul, Amanda, and Joe. Apparently, this is the formerly undisclosed law office where Paul has been taking the folks to "update" the preexisting 1995 trust and will. *I wonder why the lawyer is contacting us now after all this time.* I sit down to read. The lawyer begins by identifying himself as an estate-planning attorney who is representing our parents. He states that while working with our parents to update their affairs, he has reviewed all their previous estate-planning documents, including the "agreement of heirs" from 2007. He shares his understanding that this document was a result of "facts and circumstances" occurring many years before and that its development has led to continued family "anxiety and discord." His purpose for writing, he states, is to request "whether a discussion of the issues and an attempt to resolve them in a manner acceptable to all parties" would be of interest to us. He also declares his intention not to inform our parents of these discussions until we are able to reach some kind of agreement among the three of us children.

This man could not have caused a greater explosion in Joe and me if he had thrown a grenade our way. *Whose idea is this anyway?* The whole point of the "agreement of heirs" was to resolve the "anxiety and discord," and it didn't work. *Why should it be any different this time?* My initial reaction is not to participate. This is just going to lead to more heartache for us. Joe and I are of the same mind. But a part of me wants to see what the lawyer has to say, just in case Paul and Mom are sincere in wanting to make an agreement that is acceptable to all. I want to give them the benefit of the doubt.

"If you think you have some kind of influence," I write, "that no one else has been able to effect, we have a small window open to listen to what is being offered. But if the purpose of trying to make a different agreement is to try to make Joe and I agree to

NO LONGER A CHILD OF PROMISE

less than the two hundred thousand we formerly agreed to, then we are not interested."

The lawyer responds with a proposal. He is proposing that we accept our inheritance now, before the end of the year, under what is called a "net present value" determination. The concept is that having the money in one's hands now is worth more than receiving it ten years from now. That part makes sense.

"In addition," the lawyer says, "in receiving a lump sum now, you would be able to put this matter aside, put it to rest, and I suspect that alone would have great value to all parties concerned."

It is an interesting concept and sparks my interest until I realize that the calculations are being done using a life expectancy for the folks that is not realistic (ten years or greater) and an interest rate that I cannot obtain in today's market.

"My experience," he says, "is that a good settlement has been reached when neither party gets exactly what they want."

OK, so this IS an attempt to whittle down the original agreement under the guise of negotiating a good settlement. Joe and I have already accepted a minimal amount by signing the "agreement of heirs." Now, this lawyer wants to reduce it further. In a conference call between the lawyer, Joe, and me, we lay down our offer. I am not interested in playing this game. We will accept $155,000 each and no less. This is not about how much money we get, but about being treated as strangers rather than as members of this family who gave twelve years of our adult lives to the farm. In this same conversation, I ask the lawyer, Mr. Frost, "Why do you say that our 'agreement of heirs' isn't legal?"

"Because Paul didn't get anything of value in return," is his response.

That makes no sense to me. He got rid of the conservator. All roadblocks were removed that prevented his moving forward in any way he sees fit. Besides, I don't see how this potential agreement is any different. The lawyer is asking us to make an agreement among ourselves before approaching the folks. I also begin to realize that this is not Paul's idea at all. Consequently, if Paul doesn't like the end result, what is to stop him from going to a third lawyer? I am done with these negotiations. And so I write a final letter to the lawyer with a carbon copy to Paul.

Dear Sir:

The more I talk to you the more I realize nothing has changed … I had this hope when you first contacted me that just maybe there had been a true change of heart that was bringing this about.

The whole conflict is not about how much money we get. It is about being treated disrespectfully, deliberately being used, and then being made to feel that we are in the wrong for being angry …

If Paul feels he can't financially afford $200,000 for each to meet his agreement, a heartfelt request to us personally to be released from that would make Joe and I feel at least some better instead of this entitlement attitude that is constantly portrayed … If our (Paul's, Joe's, and my) agreement isn't legal and binding (as you say), just give us what is fair and right and leave it at that … Giving us less than agreed to without a change in heart and attitude is not going to affect reconciliation and a renewing of any relationships. It is only further promoting the hurt and injustice that has been perpetuated over the years in this family. Amanda

My goal in sending a carbon copy to Paul is to see if he has any principles in his dealings or feelings for us at all, but I forget to take into consideration the dysfunctional codependency at the farm. Why I should be shocked at the letter I receive from Mom a day later, I do not know. But there it is. It does not even start out with Dear Amanda. It just begins out of the blue.

> "The way of the transgressor is hard. I will repay saith the Lord." Amanda, have you ever read a statement like that? Did you forget? Right now I am reading in the Old Testament about the Israelites, how they were punished when they disobeyed God's commands. Satan wants to split you from living for God's way. Get back on the faith you once knew. Peace is found at the foot of the cross where Jesus Christ shed his blood for sinners. Something for you and Joe to think about. Did you forget we asked you for forgiveness for the way you say we treated you?
>
> We lie, we are disrespectful plus many others. I'm incompetent. Don't know what we are doing. You chose your own way of life to go. We didn't send you away. Now you want to run things.

I do not recognize this person who writes to me. Does using my faith against me give the writer more power? Why does she attack like this? Is it designed to cut to the core of my soul? Is it a guilt-inducing technique? Confusion and rejection are the only feelings this "admonishment" invokes. Mom goes on to quote Bible verses that supposedly apply to me.

Psalm 50: 17, 18, 19, 20 KJV
17: Seeing thou hatest instruction and castest my words behind thee.

18: When thou sawest a thief, then thou consentedst with him and hast been partaker with adulterers.

19: Thou givest thy mouth to evil, and thy tongue frameth deceit.

20: Thou sittest and speakest against thy brother; thou slandereth thine own mother's son.

21: These things hast thou done, and I kept silence; thou thoughtest that I was altogether such an one as thyself: but I will reprove thee and set them in order before thine eyes.

Read in the Bible for yourself.

I John 3: 11, 12, 13, 14, 15 KJV

11: For this is the message that ye heard from the beginning, that we should love one another.

12: Not as Cain, who was of the wicked one, and slew his brother. And wherefore slew he him? Because his own works were evil, and his brother's righteous.

13: Marvel not, my brethren, if the world hate you.

14: We know that we have passed from death unto life, because we love the brethren. He that loveth not his brother abideth in death.

15: Whosoever hateth his brother is a murderer: and ye know that no murderer has eternal life abiding in him.

I can't believe we have a daughter with such a "hard heart," especially against her family. Then try to get Joe on the same track. Follow in a criminal like Scott's ways. Steal money and use Richard Schmidt's method. Scott's trust isn't any good. Not what we intended to be … Richard Schmidt has been doing his dirty work for years to fill his pockets …

Patti told me anything we signed for attorneys while she was in her position as conservator was void …

Then you go and link up with such evil business people against your family for their money in their old age and at death. I am afraid you are the one that doesn't realize what you are doing. How do you make Gordon feel? Your pastor? Your actions may be a detriment to your job when they hear about it. As time goes on we think back that the Moorland Mennonite Church has been watching your actions and taking it out on us. So they excommunicated us.

I wonder what our relatives and friends you wrote your Christmas letter to would think if they learn what you are doing. I feel we need to start a prayer line to God to help us remain in faith and Get Behind us Satan. We all love you but not your actions. Trust you will learn before too late. Mom and Dad

I am stunned by the viciousness of the attack. My spirit has wilted beneath the weight of these biblical scourgings from the very person who is supposed to love me most. Tears do not begin to wash away the craziness my mother seems capable of throwing my way. My own mother has attacked every aspect of who I am. The shock at her ability to attack with words never seems to lessen.

I am further confused by Mom's declaration that they have sincerely asked for forgiveness for the way they treated us. When? She has never acknowledged any responsibility for any of this mess. And she has just justified her betrayal of Joe and me by saying that anything that was signed while they were under a conservatorship was not valid. Therefore, she doesn't have to abide by our verbal settlement.

But I still irrationally think that if I can just explain to my mother how I feel and how her words hurt that she will understand.

And so I write a burdened letter to my mother in December of 2008.

Dear Mom:

When Mr. Frost contacted Joe and me in mid-December, he asked us not to try to bring you into the conversation for now lest it further upset and aggravate you. I have honored that request. The letter Renee and/or Paul brought over to you was not intended for your reading. I am hurt that once again my trust has been betrayed. What purpose did his bringing you the letter accomplish?

I have erred by putting far too much emphasis on this issue and for that I am sorry. My "get it done now" nature sometimes interferes with the Lord's timing and work in my life.

Just one other request, please don't try to blame me for you and Dad being excommunicated from the church. I am sorry it happened to you, but saying that my lifestyle and behavior is what led to your being excommunicated is totally unjustified, untruthful, and extremely hurtful. I will not take responsibility for it.

I have searched my heart before God in an effort to determine what I have done on my part to contribute to this family meltdown. I feel like I am on a roller coaster I did not start and which I am powerless to get off of. Yes, I have felt my heart grow hard as my attempts to be involved and help you have been misinterpreted and judged. In my struggle to protect my heart, I have added layer upon layer of hardness to the point where I feel nothing anymore.

I am sorry that I haven't always chosen my words carefully in my hurt. I have spoken the truth, but often not in love. I have spoken instead out of my extreme frustration and lack of being heard. I am just frustrated beyond belief at the misconceptions that I can't seem to change. I realize now I can't make you see the truth. I can't change your heart so I need to leave it in the hands of God, trusting that He will bless me even though I cannot make my extended family understand my true heart. I need to let go of the family of my dreams and realize that this family will never exist.

I realize now too that I have placed the same value on my life that was placed on me in my growing up years. I have believed, erroneously, that my value was in proportion to the amount of money you were willing to pay me for my years of hard work. Therefore, knowing that you and Dad have totally disinherited me has been extremely crushing because it meant I was believing the lie that I had no value. I have come to understand that my value in God's eyes is not dependent on my parents' acceptance or willingness to include me in their will … If you just can't find it in your heart to leave anything to Joe and me, I know the Lord will bless us Himself as He already has. I have a beautiful husband and child who love me with all their heart and would do anything for me.

My heart's cry though is "Where, oh where is my mother? Why won't she fight for me or our relationship? Why does she care only about Paul? I had so much I wanted to give to my mother. I was prepared to help her with their finances, see that she got good medical care, care for her physical needs, and show her love in her waning years. But my mother no longer exists. This person says she loves me, but love is more than one sentence on a page, especially when it is preceded by four pages of words designed to justify her behavior and tear down the reader's character.

I am also the mother of a teenage daughter. I am the adult with the most maturity in this relationship, and the Lord requires more of me in this relationship. There are days when my daughter is offended and upset with me. I sit down with her and encourage her to tell me what the problem is. Often, it is something I have said or done that she is upset about. I don't just say, "You're just imagining things. You need to get Satan behind you and fix your attitude." I search my own heart to see if her words have any truth in them, apologize if necessary, promise to do better, and make an attempt to change my ways. I can't imagine how hurt she would be if I wrote letters to her attacking her character and assigning motives to her actions without checking my own motives. My job as a parent is to encourage her to find her talents that the Lord has given her and to become an independent adult in her own right, not to be offended that she doesn't want to stay at home and work for me all her life. I want my daughter to have all the blessings I can give her so I have no understanding of how one convinces oneself that totally disinheriting one or more of one's children is an okay thing. To me, that would be a total rejection of my child. I also can't imagine if she came to me upset about my behavior, saying to her, "I'm sorry you feel that way. I haven't done anything wrong so I guess that's your problem." I would, first, respond by saying, "I am so sorry that we had this misunderstanding. What can I do to make things right?" Our relationship is the most important thing in the world.

I am just really sorry that I don't have the power to fix the mess that has been created by poor choices over the years. For whatever reason, I know you can't seem to acknowledge any responsibility for yourself or Dad as to how we got to this point so there is no point in pursuing further attempts at reconciliation.

I think how Jesus was mistreated, beaten, and rejected, but He still died on the cross for us anyway. He still chose to redeem us. I ask myself if I am supposed to be like Jesus, why I can't also continue to love and give to these people who have chosen to reject me. The answer is, "I don't know, but I just can't at this time." But God commands me to forgive, so I hope with time and His power, I might be able to extend that forgiveness to you. I am mostly just so sad that I can't be the child you want me to be. Amanda

My hope is that my mother's heart will be softened, and she will respond with love, understanding, and empathy. But silence is the only response I receive over the next ten months. She does send me clippings on the necessity of forgiveness, a clipping on "wanting more than we need," and a full set of CDs on forgiveness. A hopeless feeling descends over me. I feel misunderstood. I resent that she keeps demanding that I forgive her while she offers no regrets, accepts no responsibility, and offers no understanding.

I need to resolve in my heart this problem of how to relate

to my mother. How do I maintain a relationship with her? Do I want to maintain a relationship with her? I search my soul trying to understand my mother, and I begin to draw some conclusions with the help of a counselor.

"She is not going to change," the counselor impresses on me. "Many individuals remain in unhealthy, destructive relationships because they work on fixing the other person, which requires them to take responsibility for something they cannot control. People often keep hoping that the other person will eventually become someone different. When that doesn't happen, they feel angry, hurt, disappointed, and frustrated because somehow they still expect change. You can't stop other people's destructive behavior. You can influence them and invite them to change, but you can't control or change them. All you can do is put an end to your part of the destructive cycle."

So much for my thinking that if I can just explain over and over how I feel that she will eventually understand my point of view and want to make things right. I need, at this point, to move forward as if she will never change. I need to guard my heart by staying at a distance. I need to stop talking, stop explaining, and let God take care of the result.

I often think about the Bible story of Joseph in the book of Genesis during my meditations. Joseph was betrayed by his brothers and sold into slavery in Egypt. It is a story usually used to demonstrate that Joseph forgave his brothers unconditionally, and that is what we are to do. A thought that has never occurred to me before was that Joseph, though he forgave his brothers many years before, when he met them face-to-face, did not trust them. Although he was gracious, even generous to them, he remembered their treachery and did not make himself vulnerable to them. In fact, he put them through a series of tests to see if their hearts had changed before being reconciled to them.

I begin to understand that forgiveness is one thing and reconciliation is another. Until a person take steps to change his or her attitudes, there will be no reconciliation, and there should not be.

"Dear Mom," I finally break my silence again in October of 2009.

The bottom line is that forgiveness on my part alone will not restore the relationship. Forgiveness is unconditional, and I offer you forgiveness. But reconciliation and renewal of the relationship is conditional and requires both parties' willingness to accept responsibility. The relationship will not change unless and until you are willing to acknowledge and accept ownership of your part in the hurt that has been caused to Joe and me and most importantly, be willing to take action. I need you to start standing up for all of us and not just do whatever Paul wants. And indeed I do understand that standing up for what is right for all of us by yourself is a very difficult thing for you.

I am not angry with you anymore, and I have forgiven you in my heart, but I have chosen to move on in my life since it has become evident to me that the money, the farm, and doing what Paul wants is more important to you and Paul/Renee than maintaining a relationship with Joe and me.

Love, Amanda

The phone interrupts my breakfast on the morning of March 26, 2010. I recognize from the caller ID that it is Mom calling.

"Hello?"

"Dad fell last night and broke his hip. Paul and Renee took him to the hospital. I didn't go along."

I hang up and call the hospital, as Mom has asked me, to see what I can find out.

"We are planning surgery for today. We need someone to come in and sign the consent papers."

I have always thought that I have the health-care power of attorney for the folks, but I need to go to work in just a few hours. I am on-call this evening and don't feel I can just call in at the last minute. Besides, I live fifty miles away.

"I'm sure Paul can sign them for you."

Later that evening, I receive a call at work.

"Your father is not doing well. He has been moved to intensive care. We think he might have aspirated."

I drive the fifty miles to the hospital the next day to see Dad. I am feeling like I am able emotionally to help out again without expecting anything in return. Health care is my specialty after all. I have something I can offer in this arena, and I really do care about my father. Dad remains in intensive care. His blood pressure is low and he just groans when people touch him. The pureed food from breakfast still dribbles down his chin. He refuses his pills.

Dad remains in the intensive care unit for most of the next week. He shakes his head back and forth and pushes anyone away who tries to feed him. There is talk of placing a feeding tube, which I vehemently oppose. Dad would not want this. I return a few days later to visit again. Mom soon arrives, being pushed by Renee's oldest son. Renee has dropped them off at the hospital while she goes to the dentist.

The nurses are making preparations to move Dad to a regular hospital room. As we are ushered out of the room, I notice a note taped to the outside of Dad's chart as it lies on the cart with his other personal items. Curious, I lean closer and read, "Paul (son) is to be notified of all health condition changes. **Amanda** is not to make any health-care decisions." A wave of renewed shock and disbelief rolls over me. Cold chills run up my back, and my eyes are glued on the words that assault me from the paper. So apparently, I am no longer the folks' health-care power of attorney either. No one has bothered to even mention this to me. And someone has made a special effort to make sure the nurses know that I am to have no involvement. Now I am furious. I can't believe that there is no end to the rejection. Paul knows nothing about health care.

Feeling like a zombie, I force myself to walk to the next hospital room and wait in silence until Dad is settled into bed. All I want to do now is escape. I soon say my good-byes and flee to my car. I call Gordon and pour my heart out while I sob uncontrollably. What do I do from here? I know that Renee is in Austin, so I make a decision to drive out to the farm. Paul and I are going to have a talk just between the two of us.

I stand and watch the green John Deere tractor with the attached drill coming my way. I stand in the path of the tractor. Paul is either going to stop or run over me. He opens the tractor door, and I climb in the cab with him.

"We need to talk," I blurt out. "What is this all about? Why is this note on the front of the chart? I thought I had the health care power of attorney."

He does not look at me but speaks to the tractor window. "Frost did that." He lifts both shoulders up and down in a quick gesture of dismissal. "You said you didn't want anything to do with us anymore."

So that is the justification for cutting me out. Instead of trying to reach out to me when I was hurt and angered by their actions, they just cut me out of everything.

"It is time that we stop acting like two-year-olds," I respond. "Real families make decisions together regardless of who has the POA. I try to send you gifts and make gestures toward forgiveness, and you don't even acknowledge them."

He grunts. "We don't accept gifts anymore since you wouldn't help us get rid of the conservator. You partnered with Mr. Schmidt in forcing us to pay you."

"Who put the conservator in? Who went to Mr. Schmidt for help?" I ask. "I would have to assume that you were in agreement with our contract since you signed it and had it notarized. I was supposed to know that this wasn't your real wishes?"

"Well, you got what you wanted, but Renee and I have it planned that anyone that doesn't stay on the farm doesn't get anything. I shouldn't have to work the rest of my life to pay off my brother and sister that didn't want to stay on the farm."

Okay, "I got what I wanted" is news to me, and I am not even going to ask what that means.

"Your plan is unkind and just plain wrong. It will create the same kind of animosity between your children that has been created between you, Joe, and me." I pause and then continue, "I'm glad that you get the farm, but what does it benefit you in eternity? The best thing that could have happened to us as a family would have been to lose the farm. You saved the farm, but we lost the family. There are no relationships to take into eternity, and none of the rest of it matters. I thought we were all supposed to be Christians."

Paul does not reply, and I have nothing more to say. We ride in silence to the end of the field. I get out, climb in my car, and drive home. I do not look back.

Later that evening, I make a phone call to Mom. I want some answers from her.

"Why did you change the health care POA? The last I knew I was your POA."

"I don't know what you are talking about," she denies. "I didn't change anything. I don't know why you are so upset. It's just the devil trying to make trouble."

"Don't give me the 'I don't know what you are talking about spiel.' If there was a change, you and Dad signed the papers." I shoot back at her.

"I don't really know what all I signed. We just have to live one day at a time. We'll just see what happens."

So is she purposely lying to me or is she really so mixed up that she doesn't know what she signed? I send a letter to Paul and Dad and Mom's estate-planning attorney, Mr. Frost, asking for a copy of Mom and Dad's health care directive. Paul never answers me, and Mom's attorney fires back a "Because of confidentiality issues, I cannot give you a copy without authorization from (your parents) Jay and Arlene." I have never known a parent who didn't want his or her children to have a copy of his or her health-care directives. I think that is the whole purpose of making them, so those around you know what you want for your last days on earth.

A couple of weeks later, after Dad has been discharged from the hospital and moved to the nursing home, I pick up Mom and take her along to visit Dad. I am on my way to the dentist, and my journey takes me within a short distance of the nursing home. I leave Mom to visit while I am gone. On my return, I seek out the director of nursing before going to visit Dad. I have some questions I want answered, and I am hoping that they have a copy of this health-care POA and will be willing to share it with me.

"Is there a health-care directive on file here for my dad?" I ask. "And if there is, can I get a copy of it?"

The lady sifts through the chart.

"There is one here that lists Paul as the POA ... Wait, here's a page that lists you first. I need to ask, but I think it should be okay to give you a copy." She disappears and comes back with the photocopied sheets.

"Thank you." My heart is pounding furiously. I attempt to casually walk out the door and then eagerly glance through the document. It is actually two documents. One of them is the former health-care directive that the nursing home had on file from Dad's previous admission during the time of his stroke. That one lists me as the POA. I look at the latest document drawn up by Mr. Frost. It lists Paul first, Renee second, and Joe third as those who can make decisions about Dad's health care. *My... name... does ... not ... even ... appear ... on ... the ... list.* It is like I don't even exist, like I have been wiped out of their lives! I walk out to the car to collect myself and put the document away. I can feel the depression begin wrapping around me like a boa constrictor, threatening to strangle me. I struggle to fight this reoccurring sense of insignificance and rejection that threatens to destroy me. *If my own parents don't love me and are cruel beyond belief, how can I believe that God is loving and has my best interest in mind? How can I trust Him?*

I decide that since I am here, I might just as well go see Dad. I walk down the hall to his room, but he is not there. An aide tells me that he is at lunch. I peek into the lunch room. Dad's back is to me, and I hardly recognize him. He has oxygen on, and the physical therapist is trying to get him to eat. I slide onto the stool beside him. "Hi. How are you?"

He turns and reaches out his useless right arm and then his left and envelopes me in a bear hug. He buries his face in my chest and begins to sob loudly. All eyes turn my way. *Now what do I do?* Sobs shake Dad, and he sobs on and on. I decide to do what any caring person would do. I hug him back and just hold him. I wonder what is going on in that trapped brain of his. *What does he think about? I find it ironic that a man who has been used to total control of everyone and everything has spent the last five years watching the turmoil around him, unable to even have an opinion. That has to be hell on earth.* I can't get away even if I want. I find myself help-lessly falling into his lap. I prop my right arm on the edge of the wheelchair to keep from nose-diving into the pureed food on his plate. Mom shuffles in and sits down. She does not seem alarmed at Dad's sobs but scrunches up her face at me.

"You need to feed him something," she insists.

"I can't even if I want to."

"Come on. You need to feed him. He needs to eat something," she repeats over and over.

"If you don't eat your food, Mom is going to eat it for you," I tease.

Dad's crying finally subsides, and he accepts some water, milk, and juice, but he just shakes his head if I try to spoon-feed him.

"Give me the plate," Mom says. And she eats it.

I drive home with my thoughts. The documents I got today just confirm what I already knew from Paul and Renee's actions, but somehow, the pain is still intense. *Was this Mom's idea? Paul's? The attorney's?* I have no way of knowing who is behind this cra-ziness, but I decide to try a little experiment. I have suspected over the last couple of years that Mom would sign pretty much anything that was placed in front of her. I want to see if she really doesn't know what she has signed or if she is lying to me about not knowing anything about the change in health care POA. I type up a simple letter to their attorney for both Mom and Dad to sign.

> I hereby officially authorize you, as our legal represen-
> tation, to send a signed copy of my health care direc-
> tive and my updated trust and last will and testament
> to my other children, Amanda and Joe. Thank you.

I figure since I am going through all this effort, I might as well ask for a copy of the trust too and not just the health care directive.

I have another dentist appointment a week later. I ask Mom if she would like a ride to the nursing home on my way there. I debate when and where to present the letter to her that I have drawn up. It seems easier to do it in the car and away from the farm for privacy reasons. There is another couple sharing the trailer with the folks, and sometimes the grandchildren go in and out. That and I have her undivided attention in the car. I pull into a parking space at the nursing home.

"Mom, I would like you to sign a letter so that I can get copies of your health-care directives and the other papers you have signed at Mr. Frost's since you say that you don't know what all you have signed or what the papers say."

She takes the clipboard from my hand and reads over the typed words. Without a word, she takes the pen and signs the document. I back out of the parking space and pull up to the nursing home door. I help her out of the car and into the foyer of the nursing home. I need to go on to my appointment so my plan is to come back later to visit Dad and see if I can get him to sign it. I am just not sure Dad has any idea at this point about anything. Dad is at physical therapy when I return so I take Mom home and return to visit Dad. By that time, he is ready to be escorted back to his room. I give him the pen and the letter and try to explain what I want. He fumbles with the pen for quite some time before he makes an uncoordinated line across my paper. That is probably the best signature I will ever get out of him. I mail the letter the next day, and then I wait.

I am not sure what I was thinking, but again I have underestimated the capacity of my mother to inflict cruel emotional abuse to get where she thinks she wants to go. I don't even think she knows where that is. But I have proven one thing. It does not take any coercion to get my mother to sign something. But a week later, Mom calls my husband on his cell phone.

"I am really worried about Amanda. You need to get mental help for her. She is going to get arrested for what she is doing. She is doing the same thing that Scott did. She took me out behind the nursing home and forced me to sign this paper. The judge told me not to sign any papers for anyone. She needs to have a witness if I sign a paper. I'm really worried that she is going to get into trouble."

Gordon does not know what to think. He is upset and angry with me. "I do not need this kind of phone call in the middle of my workday. Why can't you leave you mother go her way? We don't need the police knocking on our door when she tells the wrong person that you are forcing her to sign papers and 'taking advantage' of her."

I have not told him about having her sign a letter to get copies of their legal documents so he does not know the details. I have been trying to keep him out of the unhealthy relationships of my family. Mom has never called him before and tried to influence him. And it has never occurred to me that she might try to make it appear to an outsider, her lawyer, that I am physically coercing her into signing papers in an attempt to take advantage of her. I am stunned that she would twist everything, that she would blatantly lie to keep me from knowing what their legal arrangements are.

The phone rings one evening shortly after I arrive home from work. I recognize my mother's phone number. Do I answer the phone or just let it go over to the answering machine? I decide on the last ring to pick it up. Mom chatters on about how Paul has brought Dad home from the nursing home and what they are doing to deal with taking care of him at home. She pauses.

"Mom," I question, "why did you lie to my husband about forcing you to sign that letter?"

She does not deny my accusation. "Oh, I hope it didn't cause any trouble in your marriage."

"Yes, it does when you lie to him."

"Tell Gordon and my granddaughter that I am sorry all this happened. I almost didn't call you because you get so upset about all these things. You need to be calm in your job so you can take care of your patients. Having copies of our papers would just make you upset. Renee was going to write you a letter about all the steps they had to go through to get Dad out of the nursing home. I think I will just tell her not to write. You will just misunderstand it anyway."

"Mom, after this, do me a favor and don't call my church for information. And don't call my husband. Call me if you want to know something or have something to say."

"Why can't you just forgive me? Why can't we just have a nice mother-daughter relationship?" she asks.

"I can forgive you, and I have, but your behavior needs to change if we are going to have a relationship. I don't treat my daughter like you treat me. If you are truly serious about wanting a better relationship, it's simple. You can start with writing a letter to Mr. Frost. Allow Joe and me to have copies of all the legal changes you have signed for Paul in the last two years. I am not asking you to change anything. I am just asking for the courtesy of being informed and included as a member of the family. If you feel what you have done is fair and right, then you shouldn't have a problem with everyone knowing."

I am not surprised by her response. "I can't write that well."

I feel only resignation at her words. I finally truly recognize that my mother does not have the courage to do the right thing. She cannot leave the safety of her world of denial in order to make the changes necessary for reconciliation to occur. I let go of the expectation that my mother will someday be the mother that I need.

Chapter 8
ESCALATING TENSIONS

The new year of 2011 has arrived. The ring of the telephone beckons to my ears, and I hear the familiar number of my mother announced. Mom continues to call me once or twice a week. My stomach tightens every time I recognize her number, but she is my mother, so with resignation, I answer.

"We just can't do this anymore," she says to me one day in January. "All the girls have quit coming except the night one sometimes. We haven't been bathed, combed, or shaved for two weeks. Can you come and give us a bath?"

"No, I am not going to come and give you a bath. Paul made this decision without Joe or my input so he needs to own it."

"Oh, I guess we'll live through it," she concedes.

I sigh. It seems like I cannot escape this ongoing drama, as my heart strings are still tugged upon with these constant calls for help. Paul, apparently, has been hiring help through an employment agency to care for the folks. As far as I can figure out from Mom, different ones come for about a total of sixteen hours per day. Then they quit or get sick, and there is no coverage for a while.

I make the decision to drive out to the farm to talk to Paul and see for myself what is going on. I knock on his door.

"Can I come in?"

"Depends on what you want," is his comeback.

I seat myself in Dad's big desk chair in the office and turn to face Paul who sits across the room. He is flanked like sentries by his two eldest sons, seventeen-year-old Peter, and fifteen-year-old Shawn. They sit silently while we talk. I tell Paul what Mom has been telling me.

"She drives all the help away." He snorts. "I should cut off the phone service so she can't call everybody and tell everyone her troubles."

"That would help improve the situation so much," I scoff at him. "It doesn't matter what she has done. You can't just leave them over there by themselves without care. You need to start hiring help around the clock and fill in when there is no one else to help."

His lip makes an upward curl. "You can go give those baths while you're here if it's so important."

"No, I'm not going to do that," I respond. "If I don't get any say, I don't provide any care and that's the way it is."

I pull the house door closed behind me and make my way over to the trailer. I let myself in. Dad dozes in his recliner in the living room. I go in search of Mom because I want to talk to her without the ears of the other couple in the trailer hearing me. I find her in the bathroom struggling to get up off the toilet.

"I have to sit in here to talk on the phone," she whispers to me. "And nobody has come to help for a week."

"If you really want my help, I can legally get things changed so you will have help," I respond. "But you have to tell social services the truth when they come to visit. You can't tell me one thing and them another."

"Yes, yes, we need help. We can't live like this." She nods her head up and down.

As I help her back to the living room, I am jolted when I find Peter sitting demurely on a chair beside Dad talking to him. Wasn't he just over at the house? So why did he follow me over here and sit down as if he had been there all along? A warning flare has gone off in my mind, and I have lost interest in any visit. I don't come here very often any more, but I have come to realize that I am never left alone when I do. As the flame of resentment begins to kindle, I soon say good-bye and flee this place.

My contact to county social services results in a home visit, but as I anticipated, Mom declares to the caseworker that she and Dad are being well taken care of and that she is not going to have the county running her life. She is still angry over the conservator that was appointed by the court. All she remembers is that they said she was incompetent. Instead of seeing the conservator as someone who was helping her and Dad, Mom remembers the conservator as the enemy. As long as Mom continues to deny to the county that there is a problem, the caseworker declares there is nothing that they can do about my parents' living situation. The trailer is clean, and they seem well fed.

Several months go by. Since I can't figure out how to graciously totally disconnect from my mother, I determine to listen to her when she calls but not to share any of my life with her or attempt to refute any of what she says. One day in June, she calls with a request.

"I just can't see anymore. They must be able to do something. Paul won't take me. He just says I am going blind and I just have to get used to it."

I have known for some time that Mom has macular degeneration and that her eyesight is deteriorating. Paul is probably right, but that response seems rather unsympathetic to me. So what am

I going to say to her? I know that I am setting myself up again to be caught in the middle, but the loving part of me wants to help. I call the eye clinic and set up the appointment for the following week when I am off from work. I let Mom know that I will be there to pick her up first thing on Tuesday morning.

The phone call comes on Monday afternoon.

"You don't need to worry about taking me to the eye doctor tomorrow. Renee said they had this planned for a long time and they took me last Thursday. We took your name off the contact list too at the eye clinic so they won't be calling you."

I am dumbfounded. There is no apology from her—no recognition of what she has just done. There was no appointment set up for her when I called. Now I feel used and dumped. I want to scream, "You don't love me anyway, so stop trying to use me as a pawn to get what you want."

I steer my car down the township road toward the farm this August day. I have not been to visit Mom and Dad since that day in January. "Come visit us sometime," she says at least once a month, but I don't verbally respond to her invites. *What is the point in going to visit them?* Sometimes, I really want to visit them, but without someone looking over my shoulder every minute. So today, I have come up with a plan. I turn left into the field drive that leads into the hayfield behind the north windbreak. From this entry position, I cannot be seen from the big farmhouse, and I do not have to drive over the cord in the driveway that announces the arrival of visitors. My plan is to come in behind the trees and park behind the grain bins. I hope I can visit with Mom and Dad for about half an hour and then drive away before anyone knows I am here. What I am unaware of, at this point, is that there are cameras installed in several places in the trailer. I have not been here for even ten minutes when Paul comes into the trailer. I do not speak to him, and he turns around and leaves. The voices of Shawn and Peter are soon heard as they chat with the lady occupant of the trailer. The slow boil has begun in the pit of my stomach. Deep in my soul, I know why they are there. I walk into the area where the boys are and greet Shawn.

"Happy Birthday, Shawn."

He shrugs, and then his lip does an upward curl. "Why did you sneak in the back? Why can't you come in the drive like normal people do?"

My face grows hot, and I spit back at him, "Do you really want to know why I snuck in the back? Because I don't need someone spying on me when I come to visit the folks. I am entitled to visit the folks privately. You boys haven't lived anywhere else. You know nothing about the world. You think this lack of boundaries between people is normal. But it's not."

"What do you mean by that?" Shawn questions.

"That everyone deserves privacy. They're my parents too, and I don't need someone looking over my shoulder when I visit."

"I don't trust you," Shawn responds.

I turn to Peter.

"The only reason you came over here the day I visited Paul the last time was so you could see what I was going to say and do."

"I don't trust you either. I need to watch you so you don't have Mom sign any papers, take all the money, and run."

"So what do you think Paul is doing?" I counter.

"Why did you write up the trust that gave you and Joe the farm? You were mad about what he did, weren't you? It only makes sense that you would want to get even," he continues.

"Peter, I was angry, yes, and I read the trust, but I had nothing to do with making it. You're all brainwashed and have no idea what you are talking about."

"I like being a spy," Shawn informs me.

The trailer door bangs open, and Renee storms in. Without looking at me or acknowledging my presence, she orders Peter and Shawn out of the trailer.

"Don't say another word, young man. Both of you get out of here."

Her words are followed by those of Paul, who is standing outside in the yard.

"You stay off my hayfield. You're trespassing. You better leave fast because I called the sheriff."

I face him squarely.

"You go right ahead and do that. Do you know why I came in the back? Because your boys are spies. Every time I come here, they have to come over to see what I am doing."

By now, I am trembling—frightened and furious all at the same time. I have no desire to stay here. I do not even say good-bye to a mother who has no idea what just happened. I climb in the car and speed away. A sense of vulnerability pokes its head as I realize that coming here alone is no longer a good idea. It is also with sadness that I realize that the children have been included and indoctrinated into what should be a problem between the adults only. My hope that someday down the road they will come to me is a dream. Any dream of relationships here might just as well be abandoned.

"Attention all visitors," proclaims the bright-pink sign on the front door of the trailer. "As per lawyer's orders, Arlene and Jay are not allowed to give any of their possessions away (not even their

Depends) without the approval of Paul Reimer, who is trustee of Jay and Arlene's trusts. If they give you something, you must have Paul's approval before leaving the farm with it."

It is late October, and I have not been to the farm since my contentious visit in August.

I snort when I read the sign. What could possibly be of that much value that Mom can't give it away if she wants? I push the door open and enter. The trailer now is occupied only by Mom and Dad. The lady who had been living with them, along with her husband, has been evicted with no warning because, as far as I can tell, she voiced her opinion about some aspect of the care being provided to the folks. Mom has been begging me to visit, and I have been avoiding doing so. But she has been telling me strange things in her telephone calls.

"The walls have ears," she whispers. "I have to be careful what I say because the phone is bugged." Then she goes on to tell me that "Paul has taken all my stuff—our important papers, our phonographic records collection, our picture collection, and my address book with my phone numbers. He even brought me boxes one day and told me to start packing."

"Where are you moving to?" I ask.

"I don't know."

So I am not sure what is going on here. Maybe she just doesn't remember where she put the stuff. Paul is banging around in the bathroom getting Dad on and off the toilet. Outside, the backhoe idles, waiting for him to continue on with his farmwork. I find Mom seated in her chair in the living area taking a nap.

She opens her eyes and squints at me. "Oh, you're here! You can comb my hair, and then I want you to help me go through the lockbox."

She struggles to rise from her recliner lift chair and then slowly shuffles and scrunches around to gingerly lower herself onto her walker seat. As I pull the comb through her stringy white hair, Paul strides through the entry area and out the door without throwing a glance or a word my way. He has put Dad to bed before he left so the trailer is now silent. Interestingly, no boys appear to visit today. Mom chatters away as I French-braid her hair.

"I called the bank yesterday to see how much Social Security money was in our account. The bank says there is no money in my account and that no Social Security money is ever deposited there. Paul says there isn't any Social Security money."

"That is not true," I assure her. "He must be depositing the money in a different account."

She motions again toward the lockbox as she settles back into her chair. I see no point in going through anything, as I have no say in what happens anyway, but she insists. I reluctantly open the rectangular box and begin to go through the contents. At one time, this box contained diplomas, birth certificates, passports, and financial papers. Now all that I find are funeral arrangements.

"There's nothing here except your funeral arrangements."

"Everything has been messed up since Patti took all our papers. I don't think she returned them all, but Paul must have taken the ones we got back. You might as well take what you want home with you because it will be gone if you don't. I want you to take that clock with the picture of my school of nursing hospital on it," she decides.

"No, I'm not going to take anything. It would just cause problems."

"But I want you to have it. Just ask Paul before you take it."

Now I am irritated.

"I am not going to ask Paul. If you insist that I take it, I will take it but I am not going to ask my brother if it is okay. You're my mother too."

I feel smothered as I glance around the kitchen, living area, and bedroom at the cameras installed in each room. So Mom is not making it up that the "walls have ears." I soon gather up my "inheritance" of the clock and say good-bye.

"Come again soon," Mom intones.

I do not answer but turn and walk out the door.

As I drive home, I try to decide what responsibility I have in this ongoing mess and if I have any authority at all to change it. I have been taken out of their health-care powers of attorney, and I am definitely blocked from having any access to their financial affairs. I am even blocked from taking her to the doctor. My best option is to try to petition the court for the reinstatement of a conservator. It seems like the only possible way to remove Mom from the prison in which she now finds herself. But even though she tells me that she wants help, I also realize that she will probably turn on me if I try to help in the only way I can think of that would be effective. I can't quite commit myself to take that step. I am not sure I am prepared to deal with the accusations and insinuations that would follow from Mom. I can hear her now. "How can you do this to us? We don't need the government involved in our business. You'll make Paul lose the farm." And on and on. Joe and Gordon both advise me to leave her alone. She and Dad created this situation, and it is not my job to save them from it.

As I relax in front of the computer later that evening, Mom phones with a message. "You need to bring that clock back. Paul's really upset with me for giving it to you. If you don't bring it back, he is going to come and get it."

I laugh. "No, he's not. He prides himself in not talking to me so he's not going to come and get it. You gave it to me, and I'm going to keep it."

This is exactly how I expected it to turn out. And so I step back again and go about my own life with the incessant drama from Mama echoing in the background.

Chapter 9

THE PATRIARCH IS LAID TO REST

*I*n early August of 2012, Gordon, Erin, and I pack our tent camping equipment into the 2007 Chevy pickup for our only vacation of the summer. The temperature hovers in the mid-nineties. As on every other trip, I forget something. This time, I realize when we get to the camping area that I have forgotten the water jug. And the air mattress that I thought was ours is Erin's. That means Gordon and I need to sleep on the hard ground with only the foam mattresses for cushioning. Friday night starts out hot and muggy. Our German shepherd, Bella, curls up sideways between Erin and me. Bella's tongue hangs out, and her sides heave. The sweat pours off me as I lay on the ground being jiggled up and down by the rocking motion of the panting dog. In the middle of the night, the lightning flashes, the wind howls through the trees, and the water comes cascading down. The sun reappears on Saturday afternoon, and we go to the beach by the lake for a relaxing time. Erin and I sit and read while Gordon beach-combs.

As the campfire reflects off our faces in the darkness of evening, Gordon's cell phone shatters the calm. He extends it toward me.

"Do you recognize this number?"

"Answer it," I say. "It's Joe."

"Hello?"

"Where have you guys been? I've been trying to call you since this afternoon when Mom called me. Dad died around 6:30 this evening."

Our evening and our vacation have been injected with anxiety. I knew this day was coming, but I really do not want to deal with it. I dread the coming tension-filled days.

Gordon and I decide to wait until morning to drive home. There is nothing to be gained by driving home at this time of night. I have not realized before, though, how much the tension in my family has affected Gordon. We try to go to sleep in the tent, but sleep does not come. By midnight, Gordon is physically sick to his stomach and spends the rest of the night sitting up in the pickup. As the sun begins to peek over the horizon, I walk to an area of the campground where I can be alone and make a phone call to Paul. As usual, there is no answer. I talk to the indifferent machine. "Could you give me a call and let me know what the plan is?"

There is no return phone call, and since none of the three of us are sleeping anyway, we decide to pack up and head for home at 6:00 a.m. on this sunny Sunday morning that seems so normal in all other ways. We arrive home about 9:00 a.m., and my first order of business is to make a phone call to Mom.

"You've got to come and help me. There is no one here, and I can't see well enough to do this by myself. I was going through the box, and the funeral papers aren't there anymore."

"All right." I make up my mind. I decide to quickly unload

the suitcases and at least get the wash started. I leave instructions for Erin to put all our camping gear and food away.

"I know you do not like to be involved in my family's issues," I appeal to Gordon, "but I need you to go with me. I don't feel comfortable going there alone anymore."

"I understand." He nods.

We leave our house around 11:00 a.m. for the forty-five-minute drive to the farm. I try to decide during the drive if we should stop at Paul's house and try to talk to him first or just go over and help Mom. I finally decide that we should stop at Paul's first and get that over with. My stomach is in a knot, and I dread talking to him.

As we drive up to the farmhouse and park outside its stark white facade, I instruct Gordon to stay in the car. I have no idea if Paul will open the door or not, but in response to my knock, he steps out onto the porch.

"What's happening? What are you planning on doing?" I ask.

He laughs nervously. "We're meeting at 1:00 p.m. to go over things. I'm going to have the funeral in Minnesota," he declares, "and you're going to have the funeral in Ohio."

I stare at him. "Oh no! I'm not," I retort. "If we are going to have two funerals, you are going to plan them both. You have the legal authority, and you have been making all the decisions for the folks so you are going to deal with this too. I have never wanted two funerals, and it just makes no sense to me."

"Then you can go and tell Mom," Paul declares. "And I don't need you if we are only having one funeral." Somehow, his saying that does not surprise me, but it still pierces my soul.

"Is Mom going with you to the funeral home today?" I question further.

"She says she's not going along," is his response.

I turn and walk back to the car where Gordon is waiting,

and we proceed with our drive to the trailer. I find Mom alone in the bathroom of the trailer trying to clean herself up. She is disheveled. Her hair stands out in all directions. Her clothes are wrinkled and dirty, and she reeks of urine. "Are you going along to the funeral home?" I ask.

"Oh, I guess so," she mumbles.

I glance at my watch. It is 12:10. How am I going to get her dressed and to town by 1:00 p.m.? I turn around to find Paul and Renee standing in the bedroom doorway.

"Arlene, I offered to get you dressed an hour ago, and you said you were going to wait for Amanda." Renee directs her remark to Mom.

I debate in my mind as to how to remedy this situation. I just want us to do this one thing together without making a scene. I go into organized mode and push Mom on her walker out into the bedroom. I instruct Renee to get a dress that opens down the front for Mom to wear while I hurriedly comb her hair.

"No, I want that good dress that slides over my head," Mom declares. "I can't wear that worn-out one."

I am firm. There is no time for debating. "No, Mom, we are going to put on the front opening one." Within ten minutes, we are out the door and Paul is boosting Mom with his knee up into their van. Renee's comment echoes in my ears, "I tried to get her dressed before you came. I can't believe she listens to you. She wouldn't listen to me at all." Maybe my mother does still have some small respect for me as her daughter.

I climb into the passenger seat of our Toyota RAV4 and bring Gordon up to speed on what I expect to happen now. "Paul is going to drive just like he does everything else in life—at high speed. Your job is to keep up with him because I am not sure exactly where the funeral home is located."

I am asking my conservative, rule-keeping husband to break

the law in order to be a part of what should be a normal family time of cohesiveness but instead is just underscoring that we are not wanted here.

I sneak a glance at the speedometer as we hurtle past cornfields and county road intersections. The needle hovers over sixty-five miles per hour, and Paul is still pulling away from us. I finally call Erin and ask her to look up the address of the funeral home just in case we lose the hot-footed van disappearing into the distance.

Surprisingly, planning at the funeral home goes well with the physical presence of a neutral party. We are cordial and polite to each other and agree on most decisions. I, however, realize Paul and Renee have thought little about the actual service logistics and find myself being designated this task by default. How did this happen? This is not something I had intended on doing. But the atmosphere at the funeral home allows a little bit of hope to spring up in me that we will be able to bury our father amicably. And I can only conclude that I was supposed to be a part of these arrangements for only the Lord could have gotten me to the farm at just the right time to accompany this elusive family. I had no idea what time they were meeting with the funeral director.

The voices swell in a cappella singing around me as one of the Mennonite ministers I have commissioned to hold a Mennonite funeral for my father, leads the last song of the funeral.

> My heavenly home is bright and fair
> That mansion shall be mine.
> I'm going home. I'm going home.
> I'm going home to die no more.
> (From "Going Home" by William Hunter)

I had determined that I was not going to cry at my father's funeral, but slowly, I am taken back to my childhood and the church of my youth. The tears begin to slide unbidden down my face and soon become racking sobs. I am deeply saddened by the legacy my father has left behind—a family estranged, broken in pieces. Gordon slides his arm around me and holds me tight.

I had high hopes that we could, at least, be congenial to each other while burying our father after it went so well at the funeral home, but that was not to be.

Joe and his family had arrived from Virginia on Monday and settled in at the farm trailer to care for Mom during this stressful time of the loss of her life's companion. I talk to Joe on the phone on Tuesday and suggest that the three of us should get together before Joe goes back home to talk about what to do with Mom. He agrees to talk to Paul and set up the meeting for Wednesday at 10:00 a.m. This is also the day of the viewing, which will be from 7:00 to 9:00 p.m. in the evening.

I arrive at Mom's trailer around 9:30 a.m. on Wednesday.

"What's the plan?" I ask.

"We'll see if they come over at 10:00 a.m." is Joe's response. Ten comes and goes, and no one comes over. "I'm going to go over to the house and see if we can go over there and talk," Joe finally decides. He does not return for what seems like a very long time. I suspect that things are not going well. He just shakes his head when he returns.

"I guess I have to be the mediator. Talk to this one, then come back, and talk to that one. They said that you are not welcome in their home and they are not having us come over there to talk. Renee said it's too early to talk about what to do with Mom. We need to wait a few months. Besides, she said, Mom and Dad didn't want you involved in their care. That's why you aren't on the health-care power of attorney," Joe reports Renee's words to me.

I am stung and hurt. I allow the tears to come, but in a few minutes, I turn them off. What does it matter anyway? I do not understand this purposeful rejection and any involvement by Joe and me, but I can't seem to do anything about it. There is nothing to be accomplished here, so I soon head for home. The viewing is later this evening, and I want to get there on time to set up the DVD player and get the music started.

At the viewing, Joe and I, along with our families, stand in the traditional line at the casket to greet those paying their respects. Paul and Renee arrive late, and Renee stations herself out of sight behind an alcove in a room just off the funeral home chapel. Paul picks a spot toward the back of the chapel. Neither one speaks to us or approaches the casket.

The next morning before the funeral, I approach Paul in the foyer of the funeral home. Renee has already seated herself in the back of the chapel with the children.

"Are you going to sit with us? Usually, the family sits together at a funeral."

He snorts but does not answer.

"I don't know what happened yesterday," I continue, "but I just wanted to talk."

"It was already decided before yesterday," is his retort to me.

I turn and walk away. As the family gathers in the small chapel at the back with the ministers to pray before the service, the tension is palpable. We all scan each other's faces in silence, not quite knowing what to do. Renee is missing from the group. The minister finally slips from the room and returns with her in tow. She turns and faces the wall. The minister prays fervently for us, and then we all file into the chapel for the service. Paul and Renee make a left turn away from the main family line and sit in the back with their children. I am dismayed at the behavior but not really surprised. I just wonder why they think they need to make a huge statement in front of all our family and friends about how divided we are? This behavior just reestablishes my belief that there is no hope for any reconciliation ever. And this behavior is all in response to a simple request to be included in making a decision about Mom's future.

Dad's nephew, who is preaching the sermon, offers us all some advice during his talk that none of us seem to be able to apply to our situation in any concrete way. "Sometime during the last twenty years, Uncle Jay called me to talk. He was very sure that I was wrong about something. See, I have Reimer blood too, and I was very, very sure I was right. We had some conversation ..." He pauses. "There's one thing I want to say about that to all of us and especially to the family. There's one thing we have to learn in life—that you don't have to be right about everything and you can't be right about everything. We all need to forgive and be forgiven. That's all I'm going to say about that."

Later that day, after the funeral, Paul and Renee approach Joe at the farm. "We don't want you and Marilyn to go away mad," Renee appeals, her voice quiet and level.

"Well then, why did you act that way at the funeral?" Joe demands.

"I was so upset and grieving for Dad. We loved him a lot," is her explanation.

Joe does not know how to respond to that. It does, however, open the way for an hour-long conversation between Joe and Paul about the overall situation, past and present, at the farm. Included in this conversation is Paul's decision to inform Joe of what his inheritance is to be.

"You will be getting five thousand dollars per year for twenty years from Mom's trust when she dies. That is what the latest trust says."

They part with Joe leaving a challenge to Paul, "I am going to call you once a month to find out what is happening since you say that most of the things Mom is telling others is not true. That way, I will hear what is really happening from you personally."

The same grieving explanation for the behavior at the funeral is repeated to me by Renee on the phone in a conversation the following day. I graciously respond with "That's okay; we all grieve in different ways. It just would have been so much better if we could have grieved together and offered each other support."

After I pause, Renee asks, "Why do you have the guestbook and the cards with the money that was given at the funeral? Mom should be the one to open them."

"Well, the funeral director gave them to me because you and Mom were gone already," I answer back. "And in healthy families, the members would do it together, but it is really hard to do anything together when you shut me out and won't call me or talk to me."

I am frustrated by this quibbling over the smallest thing and the continued implication that I have no right to be involved, but I have no energy left to deal with this. "I will send you everything, and you can take care of it as you see fit."

The following week, Joe travels home to Virginia through the state of Ohio. Dad has been laid to rest in a Mennonite cemetery in Ohio. Joe and his wife buy a toy John Deere tractor and wagon, place a foam flower cube in the wagon, and fill it with artificial flowers. They place it on his grave. It seems a fitting tribute to a man who has placed the highest value in life on "the farm."

"Isn't it strange that the son who was the disgrace of his father is the one putting flowers on his grave?" is Joe's reflective comment.

I comfort myself with the thought that I gave my father the

Mennonite funeral he would have wanted. I buried him with love and honor, though in some ways, I feel that he did not deserve it. But then none of us deserves God's love and grace and He gives it to us freely anyway.

Chapter 10
THE ESTRANGEMENT
BECOMES PERMANENT

I tear open the envelope that arrived today in the mail from my lawyer, Mr. Walch. It is a copy of a letter sent to him in response to two separate requests to Paul's lawyer, Mr. Frost, for a copy of my father's will. I suspect that changes have been made so that there are no longer any assets in my father's name to probate, and therefore, there will not be any official filing of a will with the court. I don't expect to receive anything at this time, but I still believe it is my right to know what my father's will contains.

I unfold the letter and begin to read its contents. Mr. Frost states that the trustee (by inference this is Paul) of Jay Reimer's revocable living trust's only responsibility is to make information available to "the beneficiaries then eligible to receive mandatory or discretionary distributions of the income from the various trusts in this agreement." The lawyer goes on to say that since I am not an income beneficiary of the trust, he cannot, therefore, send me a copy of the trust without Paul's permission. Since Paul has not granted such permission, I am not to receive any information. Mr. Frost does indicate that he has enclosed a copy of Jay Reimer's last will and testament. The actual will is not enclosed but a snippet taken from the 1995 one in which Joe and I are totally disinherited.

I stare at the letter. The familiar twisting of my stomach into a knot has begun. I have just been brushed off and told that not only am I not to receive anything but that I am also not entitled to know what is in my parents' trusts. Both Mom and Paul had dropped hints in 2008 that Joe and I would be getting "what we wanted." Paul had also told Joe after Dad's funeral that each of us would be getting five thousand dollars per year for twenty years. Apparently, none of this is true. I feel totally cut off from this family, and their cruelty adds one more layer to the shell I have been slowly constructing around my heart.

I call my mother the next day.

"I have a question for you," I begin. "I asked for a copy of Dad's will, and of course, I was sent this thing that says, 'I intentionally omit all of my children from this will except for the provision made for Paul Reimer.' I was led to believe that we were not disinherited when you redid the trusts, so who is telling me the untruth?"

"Oh, I don't know anything about the will. We haven't been doing anything with it. I haven't even talked to a lawyer at all lately."

"Of course not. Dad died. Remember? When someone dies, their will can be accessed. So who is lying to us? You and Paul both have led us to believe that we're not totally disinherited. So who is lying to us?"

"Oh well, maybe you got some gossip."

"No, it's not gossip. When Paul took you and Dad out to the lawyer in 2008, you signed all these papers and you say you don't know what all you signed."

"Well, so much for this person, so much for that person, so much for that person. They try to tell me I'm senile. And the lawyer said, 'No, you're not. There is nothing wrong with your mind.' I don't know where the legal documentation is. You will have to ask Paul."

In the background, another voice cuts in, "Mother has not died. Dad says you get nothing. He was very emphatic when the lawyer asked him. I told Joe what her trust says (five thousand a year for twenty years), and Dad's gives you nothing."

"Dad did not know what he was doing in the last couple of years no matter what you guys say. Do you understand, Paul, that I would not have helped you get rid of the conservator if we had not agreed—had this agreement? I thought the whole purpose of the agreement was so that we all knew what was going to happen and we could all move on and get rid of this bitterness we have toward each other."

"I did not agree to the agreement of heirs or sign it."

"Oh, please. That is so not true. Whose lawyer was Mr. Schmidt? Was he Joe and mine?"

"He was their lawyer—Mom and Pap."

"Then why are you upset with us because we signed this contract? We signed it because we thought we had a mutual agreement."

"There ain't nothing my wishes. It was done under duress. Pap didn't want to go to Mr. Schmidt."

"But that's where you went. That's where you took Dad. And he's the one who drew up the document for you. It wasn't Joe and me taking advantage of you. You could have said, 'No, I'm not signing it.' But you didn't. That was the agreement between everybody whether Mom and Dad signed it or not—that you would go back to Schmidt and include that in the trust and will. You know, Paul, there is still the 2004 trust out there yet that is signed sufficiently, whether you know it or not. That was done while Dad was still competent."

"They revoked that," Paul shoots back.

"Who revoked that?"

"Dad signed that right quick."

"Dad signed lots of things apparently that he doesn't have any idea of what he was doing."

"He had enough ideas. He was smart enough to know that Schmidt pushed his hand to sign things he didn't want, actually physically. He was smart enough for that. Really Mom's is the only volunteer signature of anything."

"So, you're telling me your word isn't any good either?"

"My word?"

"Yes, your notarized signature!"

"On that agreement of heirs?"

"Yes."

"No, that ain't my signature."

"You think that is going to stand up in a court of law that that's not your signature? It is your signature. I know your signature."

"Well, there's no witnesses besides a wife and two parents who will be dead. It's my signature with somebody holding my arm—standing behind my back."

"Not true. That is the biggest bunk of hooey."

"That's how Pap signed his."

"That may be the way he signed his stuff, but that is not the way you signed yours."

"If you would have been the nice sister, you would have told me Dad changed the will in 2004. Nobody seems to remember him coming to your doorstep saying what you're trying to say."

"Why would I tell you something when you're not talking to me? Every time I came around, you acted like I didn't exist 'cause you've been angry at me ever since I left."

"Well, who had to pick up after you left? I wrecked my body. Now, I'm going to get screwed because of it."

"Well, you had a choice too."

"Cause this #**## Schmidt come up with a paper I didn't agree with. Held a gun to my head and said sign."

My response of, "Oh please. That is so not true," is followed by the slamming down of the phone and the silence of a dead line.

I am dazed at the slide down the slope of justification and the ridiculousness of Paul's rationale as to why he cannot be held responsible for his agreement. For a long time, I have been puzzled as to why Paul even took the folks to Mr. Schmidt if he had such strong feelings against this particular lawyer. I have finally pieced together that Paul went to Mr. Schmidt because he could not find any copies of the 1995 trust in Dad's papers. They had been disposed of. He was finally able to find the original copy boxed in Mr. Schmidt's office basement.

At first, I could not figure out, either, what paper Dad signed at Mr. Schmidt's office because the folks did not sign the agreement of heirs. It isn't until a year later when my lawyer researches who actually owned the farm at Dad's death do I learn Dad signed a paper to move the farm back into the 1995 trust so that all the assets would be in that trust—the one that left Paul everything.

I am again livid at the continued callousness of my family, and I decide that since I have nothing to lose, I might as well go ahead and petition the court for a conservator for Mom. She will get the care she needs, Paul will have to pay for it, and I will be able to access all the documents that they refuse to share with Joe and me. But before I can make a move to begin the process, Joe suggests that we should give them one more chance. So I sit down and write a letter to Mr. Frost detailing what I would like to see happen. I know in my heart that Paul, Renee, and Mom will never agree to any of it, but these are the things that need to happen for us to have any chance of rebuilding trust and have any type of family relationships. My three requests are as follows: full disclosure of all documents relating to changes to the financial affairs of my parents that have been made since the former conservator was dismissed in October 2008 (i.e., trust, wills, and estate changes); a legal document indicating that the agreement of heirs we made in exchange for helping to get rid of the former conservator is included in the estate plan as was our agreement; and a meeting with a mediator on a monthly basis to facilitate participation by all siblings in decisions about Mom's care, how much will be spent and where, end-of-life decisions, funeral plans, living arrangements, medical care, etc. Included in this would be an accounting of Social Security funds and the decisions about what caregivers to hire and what their qualifications should be.

The ink has no more than dried and the letter sent than I make the decision not to pursue anything. I know with certainty in my heart that Paul will not be open to my requests. The old pattern will emerge. He will run to Mom, which will result in a deluge of derogatory letters and calls. I really have no desire to fight the battle I know will be coming if I really would try to petition for a conservator. But the monster has already been awakened, and it doesn't take long to rear its head.

> I feel you are following the world's practices of turning your backs on the Biblical teachings that you have learned all these years. You do remember—honor your parents? You do remember in the end times the children will turn against their parents. Also, an idle mind is the devil's workshop. Prepare to meet thy God. God will not be mocked. I can't write down the verses I hear on the radio about children obeying your parents in the Lord ...

I feel that your behavior is not good for your families. They will suffer by you acting this way … You just worry about your families and forget about your wild dreams of getting our money …

I don't need a conservator. She stole enough money from us last time … Since it looks like you are going to be mean, I am going to do like Dad wanted in the start. I will have you both removed from my trust and will.

So states the letter I receive from Mom typed and mailed by Renee since Mom can no longer write legibly. Nothing has changed, and I realize I have now been assigned the scapegoat role of the family. I make a conscious decision not to respond to any of Mom's supposed letters or phone calls. There is nothing to say that will be heard. Instead, I decide to try to put the money issues aside and invite Mom and Paul's family for Christmas dinner.

I am surprised to receive a telephone call from Paul at 7:00 a.m. on a Saturday in December 2012. He never calls me. What could he want?

"Hello?" I attempt to keep my voice calm and pleasant.

"Why should we come for Christmas dinner?" Paul dives right into his purpose for calling.

"'Cause we're family," I respond.

"How am I going to get anyone else to come?" he continues on. "Nobody's interested in having any relationship with somebody who's going to force us to sell the farm."

"I'm not forcing you to sell the farm," I counter. "That's what you're feeding Mom, but that's not true."

"If I have to pay you the amount of the agreement of heirs, which I did not sign or agree to, I will have to sell the farm."

"Oh, don't tell me that. Don't even go there."

"I ain't going to honor it anyway," he declares. "Your stuff is in the trust. That's what I will honor."

"There's nothing in the trust. I have nothing to show me there's anything in the trust."

"There's stuff in the trust ... in your mother's trust."

"She just told me she was disinheriting me."

"She can't. The lawyer has deemed her basically incompetent."

"Well, she is incompetent. You and I both know that. I haven't talked to her in a month, and it's really evident to me now."

"She wants a change. The lawyer said ... well, he didn't talk to her ... but the secretaries say, all the girls that work for him say they don't recommend that anything be done."

"Yep, all you do is put information to her and you spin it around like in a blender. It comes out in pieces. Some of it's true and some of it isn't, and none of it goes together."

We go back and forth for a few more minutes, hashing over this whole situation before Paul hangs up the phone.

Over the next six months, the letters from Mom keep coming interspersed with phone calls. She sends pamphlets about discontentment, greediness, forgiveness, and something about a man who is bitterly disappointed in his children. I no longer open the letters, but the phone messages are harder to ignore. The blinking light every so often announces messages of condemnation.

> I wish you would get off of Satan's lying and try to be a little more Christian to your family. You're working like the Muslims do. I don't know why you want to run us into the country, onto the roads or what we're supposed to do. I don't know why you're being so mean. We haven't hurt you any. You'll find out when your workplace starts getting after you. By the news, they're going to be in trouble and you too. No work,

no nothing. Well, who wants to talk to someone who wants to do the worst they can think. Listen to this old Richard Schmidt. I feel sorry for Gordon and that daughter of yours how you are just doing stuff like this—illegal.

I have become numb and unmoved by my mother's crazy mixed-up thoughts. The attacks are so bizarre that I shut them out of my mind and go on with my life.

During this time, letters continue to go back and forth between Paul's lawyer, Mr. Frost, and mine, attempting to reach a settlement where Joe and I will accept $105,000 each as the final amount that we ever receive. Joe and I, wanting to just get it over with, agree to this proposal, but in the end, Paul never signs the paperwork or puts the money in escrow.

In one of the back-and-forth letters, Mr. Frost writes, "my client (Paul) is requesting your client (Amanda) return some items that may have been or were borrowed awhile back. The items in questions include Arlene Reimer's diaries and any picture slides your client has in her possession that belong to a set—including but not limited to pictures taken when they lived in Pennsylvania." *You can't be serious!* My mother GAVE me her diaries, her and Dad's love letters, and some photo albums several years ago. My mother also had many slides of her travels in Europe, but I have no idea who has them. But now, I understand that Joe and I are not only considered not worthy of any monetary inheritance by virtue of leaving the farm, but it is glaringly obvious that we also are not considered family members worthy of receiving even letters or pictures of our early years. I can hardly fathom how people convince themselves that only they are worthy of acceptance in a family. How do I respond to this in a Christ-like manner? This is so far beyond what the teachings of my childhood portrayed. Do I turn the other cheek and just give them what they want? Is that the loving thing to do? Do I just give my neighbor whatever he asks for? A few months before this, Mom had asked for some scrapbooks back that she had given me quite a few years prior. "I want to look through them again," she explained. That sounded reasonable, and since I try not to be a totally unfeeling person, I mailed them back. A few weeks later, I discovered that she had never received them. They were picked up by Paul from the mail and were in his possession. I am not about to send anything more back. I instruct my lawyer to respond. "I have no borrowed items of my mother's to return."

I am relatively successful with shutting Mom out of my life until I get an email one day in January of 2013 from Mom's sister, Sarah, who has been unable to reach her.

"Amanda, we are wondering if your Mom is okay. Susan [another sister] has tried for three days to call her and gets no answer. Susan also called Paul—no answer there either."

After leaving a message on Paul's answering machine threatening to call social services if he didn't respond, Susan gets a call back telling her that Mom is safe in a nursing home. Susan is told that Mom will be home as soon as she can walk again, but she is not told at which nursing home she is residing.

I set out on a cold, gloomy day in early February 2013, determined to locate at which nursing home my mother is residing. I am not sure what drives me to stay connected when I have been rejected over and over, but I do still care about my mother. I drive from town to town with no success. At one nursing home, I am told by the nurse that she heard my mother was across the border in Iowa. That makes no sense to me, but I finally decide to call the nursing home she mentioned when I arrive back home. After all, Mom is nowhere else that I would expect her to be. There is no hesitation from the nurse who answers the call there. She puts Mom on the phone.

"Oh, I thought you were Renee. I'm waiting for her to come and pick me up," Mom begins.

"I have been trying all day to find you," I tell her. "What happened?"

"I couldn't get out of my chair even with the help of three people. They called the ambulance and took me to the hospital. They decided I needed more help so I was sent to the hospital where you work for three days of tests."

Feelings of disbelief and anguish wrap their tentacles around my heart. She was only a few hundred feet away from me for three days and not once did Paul or Mom try to contact me.

"So whose idea was this to not tell me? Yours? Or Paul's?" I ask.

Mom does not miss a breath. "Mine. I didn't want you involved. We didn't want you to mess anything up."

I suck in my breath and pose the question that has formed in my mind, "So what you are telling me is that you don't want me to call you or visit you ever again?"

Mom does not answer even though I ask the question several times. The noose around my chest feels so tight that I think my heart will explode. I can't breathe, and I feel like I will smother. To me, this deliberate latest rejection is the spurning of the person I am and what I do best—care for others as a health-care provider. I go into the basement after I hang up the phone to sob my heart out alone. If I could just rip out this part of me that needs my mother, it would be so much easier. I make the hardest decision of my life. I rip the last shred of attachment to my mother from my heart and drown it in my tears. Erin takes me in her arms and tells me she loves me—a balm for my wounded soul. The only choice I have at this moment is to commit to never letting Erin's and my relationship go down this same path.

Chapter 11

MOVING ON WITH LIFE IN 2013

*J*ust a few days after this heart-wrenching disconnection from my mother, I board a plane in Minneapolis, Minnesota, headed for Guatemala. Several months before this, Mom had revealed that Paul had taken her to town to get a passport. "We're moving to Guatemala," she announced. A recent trip by my brother and his wife to that country is confirmed through another source so I know Mom is not making this up. I can't imagine what the attraction could be to this poor Central American country.

Shortly after this revelation from Mom, I receive an email at work requesting the participation of a certified nurse anesthetist in a medical mission to Guatemala. The team of six will be led by a local doctor. The timing is perfect for me, and the procedures planned, the repair of hernias, seem workable for someone unfamiliar with anesthesia in a foreign country. I volunteer for this adventure, which will serve two purposes. I will be able to accomplish my long-waited-for desire to serve people in a country of limited resources, and I can check out the countryside at the same time.

As we approach Guatemala City by plane, all of us are handed a form to fill out for customs. Nobody has given us instructions on what to put on this. It is in Spanish so I really can't read it. I do the best I can, hoping that I haven't declared my medical supplies wrong. That could end up causing a problem. By 2:30 p.m., we are landing. The heat and humidity just about take my breath away. There is no air conditioning here. Off comes my other sweater; the first one came off in Miami. As I go through customs, I give the customs people my form that I have filled out. I do not realize until we are lined up to have our baggage checked that everyone else seems to have a yellow copy of the customs form with them. I don't. I take Bob, our only Spanish-speaking team member, with me back to the agent at the window. Bob explains the problem, and the customs agent gives me back the precious yellow form that I need to get my suitcases through the last checkpoint. We are soon standing on the street amid honking horns and masses of people waiting for the van and pickup that will take us on the three-hour ride to Jalpatagua.

Our group stops at a Price Smart store (something like Sam's Club) to buy something that we can drink later and some snacks. I am not sure what to think of the armed guard standing outside the door and the other one in a guard tower. Is this supposed to make me feel safer or less safe? The guard in the store checks every bag as we leave the store to make sure we are not shoplifting. The talk from the driver is that violence from drug gangs in Guatemala is a huge problem and that it is not safe to be out at night.

As we travel along the narrow Guatemalan roads, the land is hilly and the road curvy. Many people ride bikes or walk along the road while cars speed by. Up and down and around we go. I notice as we drive that there are very few stop signs. It seems to be everyone for him or herself at intersections. I am beginning to think that there are no driving rules at all. The roadsides are dusty, and the people are everywhere. My nose becomes extremely plugged, and I can't breathe.

We arrive at San Juan Bautista Regional Hospital around six in the evening. I am given a room alone in the dorm at the hospital. I spray the bed and my sleep clothes with a special bug spray I have brought along. It is hot, and there is no air conditioner. They do find a fan for me. Finally, around 7:30 p.m., we are driven to the home of a local doctor for supper. I am tired and beginning to have grave doubts about being able to do this, but it is too late now to back out. I pray for God's guiding hands.

I roll out at 6:30 a.m. on Monday morning, and we all meet down at the little cafeteria in the hospital for breakfast—a breakfast of cornflakes and milk, just like at home. Then I am off to the operating room to try to get ready. The operating room has oxygen, nitrous oxide, and air hookups hanging from the ceiling for a ventilator hookup, but "they are not attached to anything outside," I am told. A large oxygen tank is all that is available to run the ventilator. The operating room does have a ventilator with a vaporizer marked with an anesthesia gas I am familiar with. I also recognize the type of ventilator from my early days in anesthesia back home and am comforted that I can maybe figure out how it operates. When I turn it on, however, and start pushing buttons to turn on the monitors, I am told, "We don't use anything electronic on it." Okay, to me, that means not much works on it. This should be an interesting experience.

The second case of the day is typical of those I do. It is to be a lady with an umbilical hernia. It will be my first attempt at doing a spinal anesthetic, as this is something I do not perform in my regular job in the United States. One of the first things that strikes me is that the Hibiclens, an antiseptic cleaning solution I am to use for prepping the patient's back, sits on the shelf precipitated out. The bottom of the bottle contains pink particulates, and the top sports a pale pink liquid. The Guatemalan staff just pour from the bottle. I, at least, decide to shake it up in an attempt to mix the product, but the particles still float undissolved in the liquid when I pour it into my tray. It takes me a little time to perform the spinal, but I am successful without any trouble. I lay the patient down on the operating room table. I turn around and scan the room. This is when I discover that everyone has disappeared, and I am alone. I go to hook up my pulse ox, which is an instrument that measures the oxygen content of the patient's blood, but the monitor has disappeared too. I turn and glance at the IV, but that does not seem to be infusing either. I feel a sense of rising panic, as I now have a totally unmonitored patient whose heart rate and blood pressure will soon be dropping in response to my spinal and there is no one but me. There is no nurse button to push and no one to fall back on. I am way too reserved to scream, but maybe that would work. I finally stick a needle into my IV bottle. That, at least, relieves the air lock and the fluid begins to flow. A Guatemalan nurse finally returns, and I point to where my monitor was a few minutes before. "Where is it?" I ask.

She looks at me blankly.

Bob soon returns and explains, "They needed the monitor next door for a C-section so they took it."

"Could you ask them to find me another?" I ask, exasperated.

The nurse disappears from the room in search of another monitor. She eventually returns with one that measures only the oxygen saturation—no blood pressure, no EKG monitoring. Well, I guess that is what I will have to live with. Once my heart rate goes back down to normal, all is well. My patient is numb above the waist, and she still is talking to me so she must have a blood pressure. This is providing anesthesia in a primitive environment.

A shower is in order after my long hot day, but as I will discover, the women's shower has no shower head and is stacked full of boxes. The second choice is to use the men's shower. I shut and lock the door the best that I can to the men's locker room. The flow of water is good, but it is ice cold. There is no hot water. I think I am about to die of hypothermia before I am done.

One day, five of those in our group travel together to Cuilapa where the regional government hospital is located. Even though it is February, the morning is bright, warm, and sunny as all the days here have been. It must be at least 70 degrees. We speed up and down hills and around curves. One of the local physicians is driving. There are people everywhere. We finally arrive at the hospital around 8:00 a.m. A long line of people are waiting to get in, as this hospital is free.

The first thing I need is a bathroom. There is no toilet seat on the shabby toilet that I am shown to, so I balance on the edge of the bowl. There is no toilet paper either. I never thought about bringing any along in spite of the admonition from our fearless leader that we should carry some at all times. We are then taken on a tour of the hospital. The hospital has ventilators in their ICUs and central lines, medication pumps, and every manner of IV drips that one would expect to see in a modern hospital in the United States, but there is no privacy. The beds are lined up one right after the other. There are men's wards, women's wards, and children's wards. The scene is chaotic and overcrowded and the equipment and beds dilapidated. Families are expected to provide the care for their loved ones. It never ceases to amaze me that the hospitals and homes are not closed in. They have open courtyards and open-to-the-air areas into which blows constant dust and dirt.

In the evenings, we all sit and talk outside our sleeping quarters in the clear cool air before we head over to Padre's for supper at eight. Padre is the Catholic priest who built the hospital and oversees its operation. Padre talks a lot about his faith and how people need to see Jesus in us. He seems sincere and dedicated to what he believes. He tells us the story of how he came to be in Guatemala while we eat. Padre was born in Malta. When he went into the priesthood, he spent two years in Italy as an apprentice. During his apprenticeship there, he decided to visit his sister in New York for about a month. In New York, he was asked to fill a vacant priesthood and ended up staying in the United States for twenty-one years. When he was sixty years old, he made a trip to Guatemala. During this trip, while sleeping one night, a rat ran over his foot. He was so startled that he prayed to God to make the devil (rat) go away. He never saw the rat again, and he believed that this was his sign from God that he should stay in Guatemala and minister to the people there. That was twenty years ago, and Padre is now eighty years old.

The end of our serving week finally arrives, and we have two scheduled days of recreation in Antigua before we fly home. I have managed to not kill anyone. For this, I thank God. We eat a breakfast of pancakes at the hospital at 7:30 on Saturday morning and are sitting on the steps and ready to go by 8:30. A pickup and a van are to be our means of transportation. I am in the van with a driver who drives like a madman. Our driver is not happy about going through Guatemala City on the way to Antigua. I have decided that the only rules of the road are "Don't hit anybody." We swerve in and out of traffic at high speed. Waiting patiently is not in the rule book either. Apparently, "use your horn liberally" is. Stop signs and speed limits are suggestions.

We arrive in Antigua around noon. All the streets are made of cobblestones. This town is much cleaner than Jutiapa and Jalapatagua, suggesting a definite tourism presence here. I decide, shortly after our arrival, that I need more money and visit a public ATM machine in town. As I walk up to it, I am surprised to spot a conservative Mennonite couple at the machine. I ask them where they are from, and they respond, "Oklahoma." I wonder why they are here, but I don't have time to ask.

The next morning, we need to be up by 5:00 a.m. to catch our ride to the volcano, which leaves at 6:00 a.m. In reality, the van doesn't come until 6:30. There are fourteen people packed into the van, including the driver. Only Bob speaks Spanish. There is one couple from New Zealand, one couple from Texas, one couple from Sweden, and the six of us. We ride for an hour and a half to the place where we are dropped off. There is more swaying right and then left around corners and bumping up and down. I am in the very back seat with Bob and Dr. Charles. It's just like riding in the back of the school bus. When we get to the park, there are kids waiting there to rent us horses for the ride up the side of the volcano. The horses are skinny and small for the load they are carrying. We get off of the horses at the top and look out over the valley below. One can see where the lava ran when the volcano erupted last in 2010. There are several volcanoes in the distance, and the beauty of the landscape is striking. This land, though, certainly is not at all suitable for large-scale farming. Farming is done in small patches on the hillsides. What Paul sees in this country, I do not know. We begin the walk back down to the bottom of the valley through the lava field. We walk for two hours over rough terrain. The volcano is smoking out the top, and I can see myself becoming crispied if it happened to erupt while we are on our walk. I realize when we get back to town that I am burnt on my forehead, nose, and neck. We arrive back in Antigua in time for lunch downtown.

We leave Guatemala City on Tuesday, February 26. I spot some more Mennonites waiting for the same flight as us and stop to chat with them. They live west of Guatemala City. I remember that there are a fair number of Mennonites in this country so maybe that is the attraction to Paul, though no one has heard anything down here about him moving to Guatemala.

I am more than happy when we land in Dallas. I am eager to see my family again. My flight to Minneapolis is uneventful, and I am home by 8:00 p.m. I am energized by my trip.

A dusty cardboard box slides off the shelf in the basement as I rearrange relics of our lives. Curious, I peek inside. These must be Mom and Dad's love letters and Mom's diaries. Mom had given them to me some time ago, but in my hurt and turmoil, I was not interested. I had shoved them out of sight high on a shelf. Now, a couple of years later, I am drawn to read them. I wonder what these people were like in their younger days. Maybe, these letters hold some answers to my search for understanding as to what happened to my family.

The love letters begin in 1953 when Dad writes to Mom and asks her if she will correspond with him. Dad is thirty years old, single, and working on his father's farm. They seem like a normal young couple, concerned with the materialism they see all around them and desiring to serve the Lord and follow His will. Mom is a mission-minded independent young woman. Her life's mission is to help those who are in need wherever in the world that might be. She is a college student at a Mennonite college in 1953, an extremely rare thing for a Mennonite woman.

As I read through each letter, I begin to realize that Mom and Dad are two very different people. Dad was isolated on the farm in a world primarily consisting of work. "Concerning your question as to other activities that interest me," Dad writes, "I must say I haven't had much time for the last ten years to think about anything else but farming. My father thought we didn't have time for other things that were not of interest to him ..." I begin to get a feeling of déjà vu. Fifty years later, I could have written those same words myself as I contemplated my own life on the farm. As I continue to read, realization also begins to emerge that Dad, knowingly or unknowingly, treated us the same way his father treated him. "You know," he says, "where there is partnership and especially with your own people and besides that, with someone up in years like my dad, a person can't do just as they feel they ought to do and would if they had all the say. I could do different and to a much better advantage with business affairs many times if it wouldn't be for my Dad. Not to complain about my Dad at all but partnership just isn't very nice to my idea and I am going to get out of it as soon as I can." In another letter, he continues, "I don't say much about those things how I feel but I don't feel that he has used me in our partnership dealings quite as he should have but I have done my part, I feel, to get things on a 'fair' basis for both of us and yet it seems to avail nothing so all I can do is just work around until things will change some way ... It almost gives me the 'blues' to think of such things but I know that life can be different if we have an unselfish attitude continually."

My own feelings and thoughts while I was struggling on the farm could have been overlaid on my father's words from his younger days. I am puzzled that in spite of this, he seemed to have no empathy and no understanding for us. What, I ask myself, causes a person to repeat their earlier experiences while leaving their own families, which they themselves found wrong and unworkable? Why would Dad repeat the same mistakes with seemingly no insight? After reading many self-help books, I have begun to understand that if we do not resolve the issues from our past and actively work to overcome them, we unconsciously pass them on to the next generation.

Understanding my mother is a much more complex issue. I

never imagined that my mother would turn on me just because I chose a different life from farming. How did my mother get this way? She comes from a rational, respectful family. Her father was generous. He gave equally to all his children.

As I read through her diaries of the years from 1943 to 1954, I see a totally different person—a person who looks a lot more like me in my younger years—independent, determined, and desiring to dedicate her life to helping those around her. She entered nurse's training in 1943 at the age of nineteen. Nurse's training programs in those days resulted in a three-year diploma. Upon graduation, she spent one semester at the Mennonite college of that day in Virginia before deciding to serve her Lord as a nurse at a clinic in the underserved hills of West Virginia. This time of domestic mission service is followed by a return home to Pennsylvania for one year. She, then signs up with the Mennonite Central Committee to serve two and a half years as a nurse at a children's home in France. My mother is described by those who knew her as cheerful, fun to work with, and always ready to help. In 1951, my mother returned to the United States to finish her bachelor's degree in nursing at the same Mennonite college where she had originally attended. It was during this time that she met my father and began dating. They were married in 1954 after her graduation from college.

I hardly recognize this person that I am reading about and am mystified as to why my mother never supported me in wanting to do the same types of things that she herself was energized by in her youth. Instead, she has chosen the opposite position of totally rejecting two of her children in order to stay true to her husband's choices. The only thing I can come up with is that she lived with my father for so many years that she became like him. She ceased to be a person in her own right and no longer is able to think or act on her own. I believe that in order to survive in the life they were living and stay with my father, she needed to convince herself that saving the farm at all cost was the right thing to do. Because of the faith that we all grew up in, leaving my father was never an option. To continue to play her role of the submissive wife and have "peace" in the household, she lived and lives in a world of denial. Denial, I realize, is a powerful tool for survival. Now she cannot admit the truth even to herself. That would mean that much of her life has been lived as a lie.

Seven months have passed since I emotionally and physically cut myself off from my mother. One day, the phone rings. I see the call is from Florida where one of my cousins lives.

"Hello," begins the cheery voice of my cousin. "Renee called and told me your mother fell again and is back in the nursing home. I tried to call and talk to your mom, but I was told that I am not on the approved family list of callers. Can you help me get on the list?"

I laugh cynically.

"I didn't know anything about this," I respond. "And I am sure I am not on the approved list either so I won't be able to help you."

So Mom is back at the nursing home again with no information being given to Joe or me. I roll this revelation over in my mind. Do I care? Should I try to go see her again? I feel nothing for her. I decide to do nothing about what I have just learned. Contact with her will only break my heart again.

Right now anyway, I am too busy planning for the trip of our lifetime. We will be leaving for an African photo safari in just a couple of weeks in October. This has been a dream of Gordon's for the past thirty years. About the time I receive the email about Mom, Gordon also becomes ill. This is just three weeks before our scheduled departure. He begins with shaking chills, high fevers, and generalized fatigue. At first, we think it is just viral and that it will go away on its own eventually. But he does not get better and I am starting to panic after this goes on for another week. We finally consult a doctor. The doctor runs a bunch of blood tests and starts him on an antibiotic for a kidney infection. There is still no improvement, and we have just a little over a week before we are to leave on our trip. A return trip to the doctor reveals that one of the blood tests hints at Lyme disease, but it was not conclusive.

"I think we should wait a few more weeks and see if the test becomes more positive," is this second doctor's advice.

"But we are supposed to leave for Africa in a week," I protest.

"You should consider canceling the trip," responds the doctor, but she does agree to start treatment for Lyme disease. I do not want to cancel this trip so I am more than thankful that within two days after starting the antibiotic, Gordon is a new man.

October 7, 2013, we board a plane for the eight-hour flight to Amsterdam, a three-hour layover there, and another eight-hour flight to Kilamanjaro, Tanzania. In Amsterdam, I have this bright idea that Gordon and I can change five dollars of American money into Euros and use it to relax in some massaging chairs. We put our five dollars into the change machine and out comes twenty cents. Seriously? What happened to all the rest? Apparently, it costs that much to make the currency exchange. Needless to say, we do not use the massaging chairs.

From Kilamanjaro, we travel to Arusha for the night. There, we meet the safari company that will take us around in Tanzania. We spend several days at the Ngororgoro Lodge while we tour the Ngororgora Crater, which is known for its abundant wildlife.

The lodge property is a beautiful place enhanced with hordes of carefully cultivated flowers. We are assigned a two-room thatched roof cabin, which we have to ourselves. Everyone bends over backward to serve us, which is not something we are used to. There are forty-eight people total in our tour group, but we are broken into groups of six per vehicle for traveling. We always travel in the safari vehicles with the same people.

After two days at this lodge, we move on to the Soroi Lodge, which is a camp in the middle of the Serengeti. All the cabins have thatched roofs and canvas sides and are built on the side of a steep hill overlooking the Serengeti. The shower is outdoors on a little deck in the wide open. It is a little disquieting to take a shower buck-naked in the outdoors, but the only creatures that can see us (I hope) are the animals on the plains. We are not allowed to go out at night without an escort to prevent the animals (mostly baboons) from getting us. On the Serengeti, we see elephants, giraffes, warthogs, lions, cheetahs, lots of gazelles, and tons and tons of zebra and wildebeests.

One day, we travel sixty kilometers to see the great migration of the wildebeests from the Masa Mara to the Serengeti. For lunch, we stop in the middle of the Serengeti under a lone shade tree. The guides set up portable tables and chairs in a semicircle so that everyone can watch the wildebeests while we eat. As everyone starts eating the box lunch from the lodge, something falls out of the tree and clunks on the table. Gordon looks up.

"There's a snake in the tree," he says.

Everyone glances up. All of our eyes follow its movements, but no one really makes any effort to move.

"We must be in the garden of Eden," someone jokes.

The guides are chattering together in Swahili. Our main guide finally shouts, "It's a black mamba, and it's very poisonous!"

Chairs go over backward and a mass of bodies flee for the

safety of the safari vehicles. The guides look over their shoulders frequently as they pick up the tables and chairs and stow them away.

"The mamba moves very fast, and a person will die within fifteen minutes if they are bitten," explains our main leader. That would be "Good-bye, everyone" because we are miles from any medical care.

Our last three days are spent at a tented camp in the interior of the Masa Mara of Kenya. I love the big tent. It is raised off the ground on stilts to keep the snakes and other vermin out. Inside, we have a bathroom just like at a hotel so it is not roughing it by any means. We can lie in bed and listen to the animal sounds outside the electric fence. At least, I hope the fence works at night because they shut off the generator from midnight until 5:00 a.m. Hmm … I wonder how that works.

I think the highlight for me is the hot-air-balloon ride over the Masa Mara on the last day of our trip. We glide silently just above the animals for about an hour on a beautiful African morning. For Gordon, the highlight is seeing all the animals. He especially wants to see a rhino. We were told that there are only sixteen in the whole game reserve in Kenya so our chances of seeing one are slim. The last day, just before dusk, one is spotted very close to the entrance to our camp. It makes for a satisfying finish. No zoo compares to God's creation up close and personal. There is no way I could have ever done any of this if I had stayed on the farm.

Chapter 12

LETTING MOM BACK INTO MY LIFE

*J*ust a couple of weeks after we return from Africa, I again receive an email from one of Mom's sisters, Sarah.

"Your mother asked Susan what she hears from Amanda. Susan told her she hasn't talked to Amanda. Your Mom then said, you know we tried to call Amanda three times when I was in the hospital but have not heard from her. Amanda has disowned me as her mother."

Well, she would be right that I have disowned her as my mother. I am still deeply wounded, and I am irate with her for not telling me the last time she was in the hospital because I might "mess things up." The words, though, seep through a crack in my emotional wall and touch that just barely smoldering spark of love for my mother. I don't believe that anyone ever tried to contact me because our caller ID keeps track of all calls attempted to the house. But I decide to give her the benefit of the doubt and make a visit to the nursing home in late October.

I find her slumped down in her recliner, covered with multiple blankets, taking a nap. She opens her eyes when I say hello, and her round face peers up at me through Coke-bottle glasses.

"Oh, it's you!" She searches for words. "I ask them at the hospital to call you. She said she tried three times, and you didn't answer the phone. They took me to the hospital—you know—where you work."

The hospital where I work! The realization dawns that for the second time in a year, she was just a few hundred feet from me for over a week and I had no knowledge of this. Renewed anger and hurt swirl around in me as I respond.

"Joe and I have been cut out of the family both legally and practically, so there is no point in even trying anymore."

"We need to forgive each other. You should call Paul, let him know you are here, and see what he says. You should go by the farm and say hello to Paul and Renee. Surprise them."

I stare at Mom's chubby little round frame that can no longer do what she wants it to do with a sense of disconnection. It is like I am outside this tragedy looking in at what seems so obvious to me but totally escapes her. Does she really not understand the damage she has done? Does she understand at all that the sense of entitlement she and Dad have instilled in Paul does not allow for actions that lead to reconciliation? I ponder a statement the Joe has made to me. "The favored child is blinded by the favoritism and damaged just as much as the spurned child." The divide between Paul and me, which she has fostered and condoned, is insurmountable. Is she really that naive? I really want to ask her what she thought was going to happen when she and Dad first drew up that will that totally disinherited Joe and me, but I don't. It would be pointless.

"Would you like to stay for lunch and eat with your mother?" asks the nurse on duty when she stops by to check on Mom.

"I guess that would be okay," I respond. I am here so I might as well spend the time.

Soon, we are seated together in a little room off the kitchen for privacy. As we eat our lunch, Mom chatters away about the staff at the nursing home and the many troubles that Paul is having on the farm. I mostly just listen. It is all so surreal. I realize by the time I leave that Mama has no telephone here. That was her favorite activity—calling her friends and family and talking for hours. Out of respect for her as my mother and with a desire to return good for evil, I place a cell phone in her hand.

"This is for you to use while you are here. You will probably need to get the staff to help you dial the numbers, but you will be able to call and talk to those you want."

She squints up at me. "I don't have any idea how to use this."

"I'm sure you will learn."

Our next month's phone bill verifies my belief that she will figure out a way, as she uses over six hundred of our shared talk minutes.

Mom begins again to call me weekly to talk. Sometimes, she complains about her care at the nursing home. Other times, she shares that she has constant jaw aches and headaches and that she can't keep any food down.

"Can you figure out what is wrong with me?" she implores. "No one here tries to help me. I just want to die and go to heaven. Maybe you could figure out which pills I should stop taking so I can die faster?"

I have no idea what to tell her. Even though I am an advanced-practice nurse, I have no information on her health from which to work. I have been blocked at every turn from being involved in her care. I finally decide to pay my mother another visit so that I can obtain a signature on an "Authorization to Release Health Information" form.

"I need you to sign this form so that I can obtain your health information if I am going to try to figure out what is going on with your health," I explain to her.

Without hesitation, she slowly signs the document, the scrawl going uphill and over the printed words on the page. She hands it back to me.

Later that evening, I receive a phone call from her.

"What was that paper you had me sign today? I need to know so that I can tell Paul."

"Don't you dare tell Paul," I explode at her. "You are just going to make trouble."

So she can't even remember for eight hours what she signed. I have also pieced together from the nursing home staff that the things she says about them leaving her to sit for hours at a time are untrue. To her, an hour seems like all day.

Early on a Saturday morning just three short months later, I receive a phone call from the nursing home.

"Your mother was taken to the hospital a few minutes ago. She is in heart failure or maybe in cardiac arrest."

I pause for just a moment. "Thank you for letting me know."

I had left a message with the nursing station at the nursing home during my first visit that I wanted to be called if anything ever happened to Mom. Otherwise, Joe and I expected that our mother would be dead and buried before we even knew about it.

It is eighty-five miles to the hospital where they have taken Mom. I debate with myself whether I should even try to go, as I am sure that I will be too late anyway. But I gather up myself and make the drive. Mom is still in the emergency room when I arrive but not coherent. Even though it is an hour since I got the call, I am the first family member to arrive. Mom is gasping for air and does not respond to my voice when spoken to. Paul and Renee, with the children in tow, appear in the doorway within fifteen minutes of my arrival. Only Paul and Shawn, the second son, come into the ER cubicle.

"We need to move her to a different hospital if we are going to help her breathe," the ER doctor says to us. "We do not have any ventilators here."

"She wouldn't want that." Paul and I both respond together. We shake our heads back and forth. At least we agree on that.

"I'll be back tomorrow to see how she is doing." Paul throws the words over his shoulder as he disappears out the door and down the hall.

I am left alone with the doctor.

"Maybe we could start some dopamine or dobutamine to help her kidneys then," the doctor continues.

As a nurse who has worked in intensive care for years, I know what he is talking about. "No," I respond. "I just want you to make her comfortable. She is a do not resuscitate, and she made it very clear in the last couple of months that she just wanted to die and go to heaven."

I wonder how it is that in spite of not officially having any legal authority to make health-care decisions for my mother, I am the one standing here alone, making this final decision. I fully expect that my mother will take her last breath in the next twenty-four hours, but she doesn't. She lingers on. As Joe and I sit with her over the course of the next two weeks, I wonder why it has to end this way. What is the purpose of this slow dying process during which there is no possibility of exchanging words? My heart is accepting that there will never be any reconciliation. In my limited way, I have forgiven my mother, but I still find it difficult to be touched by her last days. The part of me that was her daughter died with her rejection of me as a person worthy of equal value to that of the son who stayed on the farm.

On the second Sunday of our vigil, as Gordon and I arrive to sit with her, I touch her forehead and stroke it. She lifts her arms off the covers and starts to thrash around and moan. *Maybe I should just not touch her.* I elect to go around the bed and sit quietly beside her for a few minutes. Then, I take her gnarled fingers in my hand. This starts the restless thrashing again. I wonder again if it would be better not to touch her, but as I withdraw my hand, she seems to purposefully reach for it. I take her hand and hold it while she falls asleep.

During these two weeks while Joe, his wife, my husband, and I sit with Mom, Paul does not come by to visit. I try to set up a family meeting through social services, but Paul never shows up at the time requested. I have no idea how to deal with a funeral. I don't even know if there is going to be a funeral, and at this time, I am still ambivalent about going to her funeral. How can we bury our mother when we can't even speak to each other? I do not want a repeat of the behavior at our father's funeral.

The phone explodes the quietness of the night on a morning in early April 2014.

"Your mother is breathing only two to three times a minute. Do you want to come?"

I wrestle with myself. It is 3:00 a.m. Should I go? With the distance to the hospital, I will never get there in time. But in the lonely, empty darkness of early morning, I make one last drive to the hospital. Mom's body lies cold and still by the time I arrive, released at last to her eternal destiny. I sit with her for a long time as I try to sort out what to do next. Joe's and my phone messages to Paul have gone unanswered over the last week. We cannot even visit the farm to talk without his permission, as a locked gate needing an access code has been erected since Mom was moved to the nursing home.

"What should we do with your mother?" is the question of the nursing home staff.

I have no authority to give them any direction, but I can't just leave them hanging. "Give Paul another hour and try to call him again. If he still doesn't answer, just send her to the City Funeral Home in Mankato. That is where their prior arrangements were made."

As I drive home, I wonder how to proceed from here. I decide to drive by the farm and see if I can try to talk to Paul person to person. But the question remains, how am I going to get through the gate at the end of the drive. As I drive down the gravel road that leads to the farm, a milk-tanker semi pulls out in front of me. *I wonder if this truck is going to the farm.* As I follow the truck, sure enough, the driver pulls into the farm driveway, hops out, and enters the code into the digital box. As the gate swings open, I see my chance. *Well, I guess the Lord opened the gate. I guess that is my sign to enter.* My heart pounds 150 beats per minute as I begin my search for my brother. No one is in the barn, the folks' house trailer door is locked tight, and no one answers when I call out "H-e-l-l-o" into the main house door. Holding my breath, I gingerly tiptoe through the entryway, the kitchen, on through the living room, and into the office. The only thing that greets me is silence. *Strange!* Someone is always at home here. I must have passed them on their way to the hospital while I was on my way here. Suddenly, it dawns on me. *I need to get out of here before I get locked in when the milk truck leaves.*

As I relay this story to my husband, Gordon, later that evening, he stops and gazes at me. "You didn't," he says. "What if they had cameras in the house?"

Oops! I never thought about that possibility.

Two days after Mom's death, I leave one more message

begging Paul to contact me so that Joe and I will know how to plan. He finally calls me back.

"What is the plan?" I ask.

"There isn't a plan. I am going to maybe have a viewing, but that is all. You guys can do what you want. Mom said we should just bury her," he responds.

"She might have said that, but I don't think she actually meant that," is my comeback to him. "And by the way, are you going to have any pictures?"

"No, I don't have time for that."

"Do you care if I have some pictures?"

"I don't care what you do."

"When are you meeting to plan things?"

"Tomorrow."

"Do you care if I come?"

"Everything is all done already. There are just a few papers to sign."

Well, it is the usual not being included as part of the family, but this time, I don't care. I am going to get some pictures together for a slide show at the viewing. When I tell Joe what is happening in Minnesota, he decides to move ahead in planning for a funeral in Ohio where Mom is to be buried beside Dad. The problem is how does one plan a funeral when all the people who could potentially participate in the service have been alienated by my parents? Whom will we ask to lead the singing, to preach the sermon, and to do the graveside service? And I still have not decided if I will personally attend.

The clouds hang heavy in the dark sky, and raindrops splatter the open-sided tent that has been erected over the grave site. A

group of about forty family and friends has gathered with Joe and
my families in Ohio to say their final good-byes to my mother. I
gather my coat closely around myself and shiver as the cold wind
sweeps over the six men and Joe's young son who slide the casket
above its final resting place. Pools of water build behind my eyelids as music starts to mix with the mournful wind of this dreary
day. My mortally wounded heart does not allow me to cry for the
loss of my mother. But a recording of Joe's daughter playing "The
Sands of Time Are Sinking" on the keyboard fills the silence and
pours a balm over the crust on my soul. Then, the music changes
to a CD as the casket is lowered into the cold ground to its final
resting place.

> We gather together to say our good-byes
> To our precious loved one, oh how our hearts ache
> inside
> Then we went to the place, where they lowered their
> body down,
> Some call it grave. I call it resurrection ground.
> (From "Resurrection Ground" by Mark Dibler)

I am glad that I made the decision to come here today. I cannot change what has now become permanent, but I feel like Joe
and I honored our mother the best that we could. I have come to
understand in a small way that my mother, in her last few years,
was not totally responsible for her behavior, though it was certainly still devastatingly hurtful, as dementia is one of the final
diagnoses listed on her death certificate.

Joe and I had agreed to hold the funeral on a Monday in
mid-April 2014 in Ohio. This gave me and Gordon time to drive
out and back before I needed to return to work on Wednesday.
A decision was made to ask members of Joe's wife's family and a

brother-in-law of Mom's to officiate at the funeral. The support from Joe's family is touching. This, along with the support of some of Mom's sisters and their families, makes for a service that blesses Joe and me. Joe, in his desire to also honor our mother, writes a poem that express the feelings of both of us, and he reads it during the service as his farewell.

If You Only Knew

If you only knew the labor that those
twisted hands have endured
Feeding calves and mending clothes, so her
lover's dreams would be secured.

If you only knew the miles those swollen feet have trod,
Committed to the service of a tiller of the sod.

Then you would comprehend, our mother "died" long ago!
Her life was lost in the wishes of others,
so their desires she would know.

Those lips that now lie silent, how often have we heard:
That "right is right and wrong is wrong,
you'll find it in God's Word."

No, Mama was not perfect. Forgiveness came hard, this is true.
Lord, grant us compassion to understand,
that she did the best she knew.
(Joseph Reimer, 2014)

Chapter 13

THE AFTERMATH

*M*om's funeral is over, and Joe and I return to our lives, wondering if Paul will include us in settling the estate by paying out what he has said Mom left in her trust or make an attempt to satisfy the agreement of heirs. We hear nothing from Paul, and one day, I decide to drive by the farm. Now in addition to the code-locked gate blocking the main driveway, short concrete barriers have been installed across various field driveways. Interestingly, it appears that an addition twice as big as the main house has begun to spring up as well. I find it hard to understand the paranoia being evidenced by my brother, but I also realize I cannot fix what has been broken and deteriorating for a very long time. I am no longer angry with him and his wife, but I do still feel that he needs to be held accountable for the commitments that were made.

A decision is made to have my lawyer send a letter to Mr. Frost, Paul's lawyer, requesting a copy of Mom's will and trust. A month goes by with no reply. Finally, another letter is sent. My lawyer is requesting that a copy of the will be sent immediately or filed with the court. If this does not happen, he will be commencing probate, seeking my appointment as personal representative so that I can gain access to the will, the trust, and any other pertinent documents.

I am sure that Paul and Renee will never stand by and allow me to become the executor of the estate—that much I know. Mr. Frost does wait a full month until the deadline given to him and Paul before sending his response, "Enclosed for filing is the original last will of Arlene Reimer." Mr. Frost, however, does not include a copy of the trust. I eagerly read through the will. I really want to know if what Paul has been telling us is true. But if I thought I was going to learn anything of value, that is not to be.

"All my property of whatever nature and kind, wherever situated, shall be distributed to my revocable living trust ... All of my property shall be disposed of under the terms of my revocable living trust."

Paul and his lawyer have repeatedly refused to share a copy of the trust with us, so Joe and I know nothing more than we did before. It is not that I expected anything different from my older brother, but my soul still swirls in confusion and an inability to understand how one's family can so purposefully and deliberately reject those they are supposed to care the most about. The question that comes up repeatedly for Joe and me is, "What are they hiding that the trust is an unshareable secret?"

One day, while vacationing in Yosemite Valley, California, I notice an icon on my cell phone indicating that I have a message. *I wonder who could be calling me.* I rarely receive calls on my cell phone. The number is a Minnesota number, so I decide to check it out.

"This is Sam Hovda," says a man's voice. "Could you give me a call when you get a chance?"

That's interesting. Mr. Hovda is the gentleman who has been managing the folks' financial investments since the savings embezzled by Scott Hanson was returned to them by Mr. Hanson's company.

Curious as to what he wants, I find a spot with one bar of cell phone reception and return his call.

"Hello. This is Amanda. I just got your message."

"I have been talking to Paul," he begins. "I think I have been able to talk him into giving you and Joe some of that money he promised you. He was going to fight you to the very end, and I told him he can't do that. I told him you guys worked for that money and there is no question that you deserve it. I said, 'Paul, you need to settle this. You have only one brother and sister, and this is not good for your children. You need to settle this so you can sit down and have a picnic together as a family.'"

"I am not sure that is ever going to happen," I respond, "but thank you for trying to help."

"What do you need to settle this thing?" he questions.

"At this point, I would be willing to accept a hundred thousand as settlement for the agreement of heirs with the understanding that we also receive a copy of the trust and the five thousand per year for twenty years that he said was in there."

"All right," Mr. Hovda concludes the call. "I will call you back when I get it all worked out with Paul."

After our return from California, I also send a letter to Paul, detailing the acceptable options that I have communicated to Mr. Hovda. I end that letter with a plea: "PLEASE, PLEASE consider settling this without a bunch of court costs and legal exposure. Then you can go about your business and live your life as you desire. I know you have no desire to forgive me and I can't make you forgive me and move on. I have forgiven you for what I see as your and Mom's betrayal of us in not honoring our agreement, and I also ask that you let go of the belief that we somehow betrayed you by signing the agreement of heirs. Let's just follow through with the commitments we made like adults and move on. Thank you."

A week later, Mr. Hovda calls me back. "It's all set. Paul wrote two one-hundred-thousand-dollar checks, and I have them here at my office. He just wants you to sign a paper for him, and he will send the money. There is no lawyer involved."

I am happy and excited that we are resolving this so easily when just a year and a half ago, this same type of agreement through the lawyer had fallen through. Why I should think it would be amicable and easy, I don't know. A few days later, an envelope arrives in the mail from Paul and Renee's address. In it is a two-and-a-half-page agreement with nine points that Joe and I are supposed to sign and return in exchange for the money. We are agreeing to a lesser settlement of the agreement of heirs. We are agreeing that the farm shall belong to Paul, and there are nine lines of conditions under which we agree to never ever, now or in the future, seek any compensation in regards to our agreement of heirs. My head is spinning by the time I finish reading this. Is all this really necessary? Even though, supposedly, no lawyer is involved, the language and terminology comes right out of the agreement that Mr. Frost had wanted us to sign in 2012 in exchange for the elusive $105,000 payout proposed at that time. I feel like the batted around figurine in an emotionless game of cat-and-mouse. I certainly don't feel like a member of a family who is getting what I worked for and was promised.

Since Paul is not signing this document and this is what I am agreeing to, I decide to modify the document to include my expectation (which has not been acknowledged here anywhere) that Paul will still give us a copy of the trust, which we are legally entitled to and distribute to me and Joe whatever the trust stipulates in addition to this one half of the notarized agreement of heirs amount. A few more days pass before I receive another envelope containing an unsigned letter and a copy of another similar agreement sent to me to sign. Paul and Renee have upped the ante in that they are offering $115,000 to settle if Joe and I sign within three days. For every day we wait, the amount goes down until after one week, the offer is no longer valid.

"If you do not return the enclosed updated copy of the release (signed, notarized, and **unaltered**), the checks written to you both will be voided. Also, there will be no back and forth negotiations, no phone calls, no emails, no letters, and no coming to the farm to 'talk.' This is a here it is, take it or leave it thing."

How much more inflexible, hard-hearted, and cold can one be? I understand perfectly that the message is, "If you don't play by our rules, we will make sure you do not ever get anything." And I also understand perfectly, by this point, that I am not considered to be of any value to my brother. There is no point in holding onto some belief that he might want to do the right thing. I am going to take whatever money he is offering. Against my lawyer's advice, I sign their paper and return it. I also write a note asking Paul to please "set aside the power trip for one moment and send Joe his share of the money anyway. I am sure he will sign the document for you after he receives the money."

A few days later, I receive my $115,000 check. Joe continues to refuse to sign the document. He is angry that Paul is manipulating us and trying to buy us off so that he doesn't have to pay what he agreed to. To no avail, I try to talk Joe into signing the agreement and get at least something so that we can lay this to rest. But he believes the principle is more important. He believes that Paul needs to give the money to him of his free will out of a heart of caring for us.

I tell Joe, "That is never going to happen. You need to get that idea out of your head. Paul does not have any empathy or caring for us."

I no longer have any hope that the love of Christ for us might still be somewhere in Paul's heart. In fact, just a few months later, when Joe again asks Paul for a copy of the trust, Paul reveals that he has turned the trustee position of Mom's trust over to an off-shore account in the Cook Islands. He did this just four months before Mom's death while she was in the nursing home, making any and all assets unavailable to us.

My mind takes me back to the words I wrote to Paul in 1995 when he was struggling with feeling like he was missing out on life and being taken advantage of on the farm. "If you wait until the folks are gone to do the things you want, the best part of your life will be gone by then and the bitterness you feel will be hard to get rid of." I could never in a million years have seen how prophetic my words were to become.

As my husband and I drive up to the funeral home in October 2014, the parking lot and every street surrounding the building is full of cars. We have come to the viewing of Alvin Schmutz, the minister of the Moorland Mennonite Church, the church of my youth. His death, at seventy-five, was sudden, a surprise to all. I have maintained a friendship over the years with his daughter, Yolanda Schowalter, who along with her husband provided me with the room to live in during that first year after my departure from the farm. I wanted to be here for her, her sisters, brother, and mother, but I feel like a stranger in a strange land. I no longer recognize people I knew twenty years ago. One man I do recognize is the former bishop, Saul Schowalter. He gives me a big hug and welcomes me warmly. He is now eighty-four years old. As we chat, he apologizes several times for those years so long ago when I lived on the farm and we were all denied Communion by the church in response to our father's behavior and attitudes.

"I just didn't know what else to do and how to treat the situation differently. Your father just didn't listen to anything."

"You think I don't know that?" I reassure him. "I understand all too well that my father did not listen to anyone. I hold no ill feelings toward you or any of the ministers for how it turned out with the church."

Even though I harbor no animosity toward this spiritual leader, it is still tremendously healing to hear those words of humility so many years later. I realize, too, how caught I was between loyalty to my father and what he wanted and wanting to behave differently. It was just not possible in that situation. How I wish Paul, too, could understand that we were all victims of our father's control and expectations, as, I believe, that understanding is the key to any possibility of ever being reconciled to each other. I will always be open to reconciling with Paul, but I really don't see that ever happening. Our hearts have become too hard.

Joe makes the decision over the summer to pursue, through a lawyer, a petition with the court for an accounting and a copy of Mom's trust. This is something that beneficiaries of any trust are entitled to. "If it takes me until I die, I am going to find out what is in that trust that is such a secret," he declares. For me, it is over, but I also want to support Joe.

The court date is set for late February 2015 at 2:00 p.m. The day dawns cold but sunny. The bundled-up digital man thermometer on our wall declares the temperature to be -15 degrees.

Joe had flown in the day before and settled into the section of our house previously occupied by our daughter. The thought never occurs to me, but her closet no longer contains any personal hygiene items. Due to my busy day and preoccupation with life, I had not supplied my brother with any such items. As a result, Joe had a pronouncement to make after taking his evening shower.

"My wife didn't put any shampoo into my bag so I looked through your closet. All I could find was dog shampoo so I used it. I get treated like a dog so I might as well act like a dog."

I could not suppress the chuckle that escaped my lips. "You're so funny, Joe."

We make the drive to the courthouse through what we would call a ground blizzard in Minnesota. The snow is driven across the road by the howling wind, making visibility low and the road treacherous in spots. We are not expecting Paul to be there. His lawyer has communicated to Joe's lawyer that they will not be attending the hearing because, as far as they are concerned, there is no defense needed for their argument. Their position is that we are not beneficiaries of either Mom's or Dad's trusts so we are not entitled to copies or an accounting of the trusts. That is how the law reads in regards to trusts. Both Joe and I find this to be a puzzling argument. Paul specifically told Joe at Dad's funeral that we would be getting a hundred thousand over twenty years from Mom's trust. "So what happened in the year and one half after Dad's death that changes that?" is our question.

About ten minutes before the hearing is to begin, an average-height, thin woman dressed in a professional pantsuit appears. "I am here as counsel for Paul Reimer," she identifies herself to the bailiff.

I poke Joe in the ribs and turn toward him. "That's Paul's lawyer. I thought they weren't coming."

We enter the courtroom, and all rise for the judge's entrance. Joe's lawyer argues during the hearing that we have no way of telling if we are beneficiaries if we cannot see the documents. Paul's lawyer argues that Paul is no longer the trustee and that we are not beneficiaries. The judge's eyebrows twitch upward for just a moment when the answer to his question about who is the current trustee is answered with, "Seldom Trustees, an offshore trustee account, in the Cook Islands." After thirty minutes of discussion, the judge does rule that Paul has to give our lawyers copies of all the trusts that he has. Before we even leave the courtroom, Paul's lawyer hands over the last two amendments made to Mom's trust.

The first amendment we receive is the document made in 2008 when Paul took Mom and Dad to Mr. Frost after the termination of the conservator. It is the part of the trust that we have never seen in which Mom leaves us the a hundred thousand dollars each over twenty years. The second amendment is a document drawn up and signed in late June 2013, just a few short months before her death. It is signed by both Paul and Mom and "reinstates the intent of certain provisions from Article II, paragraph C and Article VII, paragraph G of my original trust document."

I page back through the original document, and there it is:

> At the present time I have the following children: Paul Reimer, Amanda Reimer, and Joseph Reimer. I intentionally omit all of my children from this my Last Will and Testament except for the provisions made for Paul Reimer as set forth herein. The omission of all of my children except for Paul Reimer is not occasioned by accident or mistake and is intention. My son, Paul Reimer, has stayed with us on the farm

and we would not have been able to hold it together
and have the type of assets we have today without his
dedication and assistance. He is the one that should
reap the benefit of his hard work ... All of my clothing, jewelry, ornaments, automobile or automobiles,
books, household furniture and furnishings, and personal effects of every kind and nature used about my
person or home at the time of my decease I hereby
devise ... the same in equal shares to my son, Paul
Reimer, and the issue of my son, Paul Reimer, by right
of representation ...

I feel like I have been backhanded with a blow so powerful
that I am unable to maintain my balance. I thought I was beyond
being hurt and shocked by any actions of those in my family, but
I stare at the papers in front of me. I wonder if Mom really knew
what she was doing in her state of mind. Did she really know
what the document said? And if she did, did she really hate us
that much? I am stunned by what I have just learned. I don't know
what to think. My thoughts swirl around in one jumbled mess,
and I struggle to understand this final rejection. I thought I had
moved on, and here it is slammed back in my face. My world reels
and I struggle to resurface.

Now, I understand why Paul has been avoiding us through the
time of Mom's dying, her funeral, and ever after. His intention
was to hide this from us forever by simply ignoring us.

I think back to a time when I was nine years old and Paul
was eleven. I came across Paul and Dad kneeling in the barn by
a hay bale, praying together as Paul accepted Christ as his Savior.
"I want to do that too," I exclaimed to my father. Hence, Dad
led me too in praying to accept Christ as my Savior. I looked up
to my big brother and wanted to follow his footsteps. He was

my protector and my hero. So how does one get so far from the Christian teachings of the Bible about love, forgiveness, and going the extra mile that we all learned as children in the Mennonite church? How have we allowed our hearts to become so hard that we have permitted a piece of property that we can't take with us from this life to turn us from friends and siblings into enemies? With sadness, I realize that the distorted beliefs of my father have infiltrated into the value system of all three of us and initiated a downward spiral that led to us placing the farm above family relationships. In Matthew 19:17 (KJV), the rich young ruler asks Jesus, "What good thing shall I do that I may have eternal life?" After Jesus tells him to keep the commandments and honor his father and mother, which he indicates that he has done, Jesus touches the young ruler's heart attachment to his possessions. "If thou wilt be perfect, go and sell that thou hast, and give to the poor, and thou shalt have treasure in heaven: and come and follow me." (Matthew 19:21 KJV). And the young man goes away "very sorrowful: for he had great possessions." The young man cannot embrace the greater good Jesus has for him in relationship because of his misplaced affections.

I lay on the wood slatted front porch of our house with the warm March sun touching my face and filling me with comfort and peace. I whip the tennis ball out over the yard for the dog each time she brings it back to me as I mull over the whole situation. She knows just where to place the ball by my hand so I don't have to move.

Being upset by all this is ridiculous. I am a grown woman with a great husband, a beautiful daughter, and a professional career. My husband and I are financially stable. Everything in this world that my husband and I own we have earned with our own hands, and I am proud of that. God has blessed us with more than we need and much more to give to those who don't have enough. I would never exchange the years of being able to follow my dreams and to travel for wasted years of servitude under my father's patriarchal control while hoping that "someday you will get something from this farm." I don't need the money, and I refuse to make my earthly possessions my first priority over the relationships I have with those I love.

In the final analysis, I am blessed by the maker of the universe. I am a person loved by God in my own right, and He forgives me no matter what I have done if I will only ask Him. I am sure that my Heavenly Father has a mansion waiting for me in heaven, as He always keeps his promises to us and welcomes us into His family even if our earthly family has disowned us. And I do have one loyal friend from this biological family here on earth, my brother Joe. The rest of this broken mess I turn over to God for His handling.

Epilogue

$\mathcal{D}$ear Reader, if you see yourself in any of the dynamics of this story, please stop and consider where your actions might lead. Is losing your family really worth holding on to the money, the control, or the business you have created? Sometimes, the older generation feels justified in punishing their children through the will for things done or not done that they did not agree with. But they fail to consider the enmity that this will most likely create between their offspring once they are dead and gone. Yes, the law says people have the right to leave their possessions to whomever they see fit, but not treating all of one's children fairly in some way is a sure way to destroy the family. If the relationships of only one family can be saved by the sharing of this heartbreaking story, this heartbreaking part of my life will be of value.

Questions to Consider

1. Where did it all go wrong in this family? What were the underlying beliefs that set this family up for a lack of understanding and forgiveness of each other?

2. How would you have resolved this situation differently? Would your choice have made a difference in the outcome?

3. What biblical values are violated by Dad? Mom? Paul? The Writer?

CPSIA information can be obtained
at www.ICGtesting.com
Printed in the USA
FSOW01n1944010416
18754FS